IMAGES
of America

GLEN CARBON

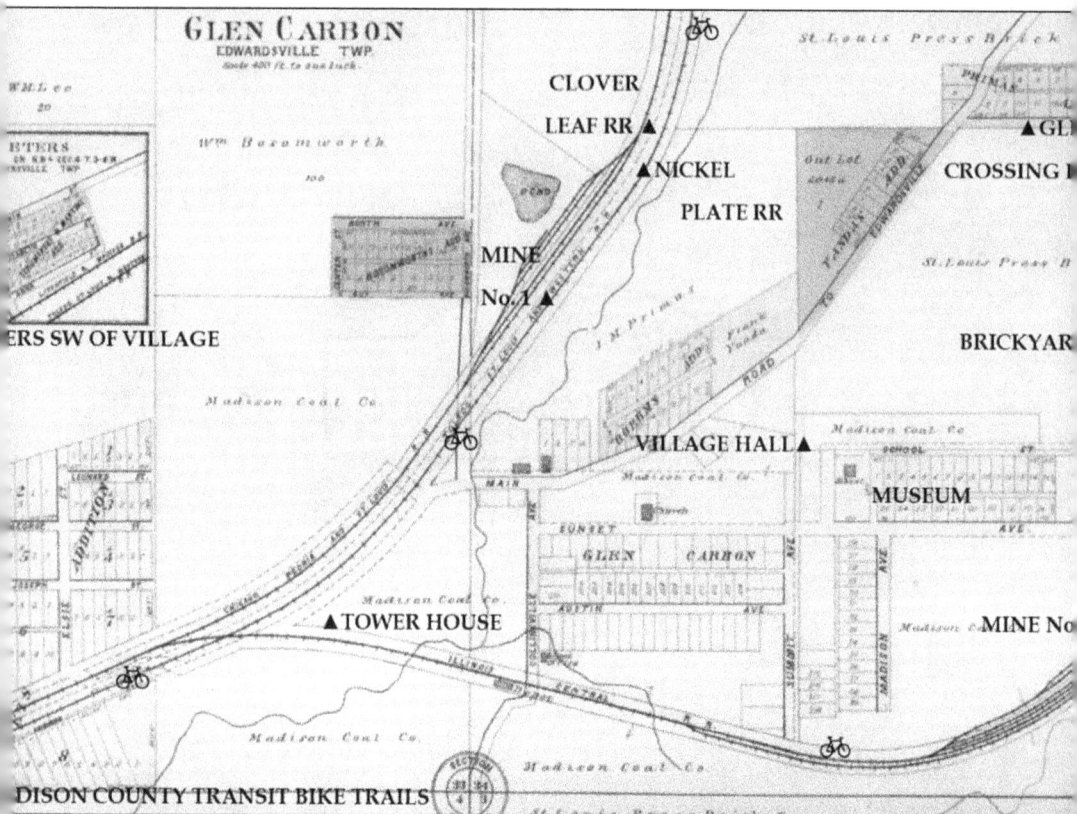

This is a 1906 plat map of Glen Carbon, Illinois. A two-mile Main Street, centrally located, unites the turn-of-the-century village. The map shows Judy Creek, three railroads (the Clover Leaf, Nickle Plate, and Illinois Central), the brickyard, Mine Nos. 1 and 2, and the village hall and museum. Bicycles indicate that the railroads were turned into bike and hiking paths that are now part of the Madison County Transit system. Main and School Streets, Sunset and Austin Avenues, and Glen Crossing Road run east and west; Collinsville, Summit, and Madison Avenues run north and south. Northeast Main Street is 30 feet higher at the Glen Crossing intersection than at the Collinsville Avenue intersection. Before the brickyard and coal mines were built, the bluff hillsides were wooded. (Courtesy of the Glen Carbon Heritage Museum.)

ON THE COVER: Seen here is the surface area of Madison Coal Corporation Mine No. 2 in the village in 1907, with workers, visitors, and a mule. Mules were used below ground to haul coal cars. Coal miners from all over the world came to the village to work. Approximately 6,000 men worked in the Glen Carbon mines from 1895 until 1931; some worked for a week, and some worked all their lives. Their descendants live here today. (Courtesy of the Glen Carbon Heritage Museum.)

IMAGES
of America

GLEN CARBON

Joyce A. Williams

ARCADIA
PUBLISHING

Published by Arcadia Publishing
Charleston, South Carolina

Library of Congress Control Number: 2021946224

For all general information, please contact Arcadia Publishing:
Telephone 843-853-2070
Fax 843-853-0044
E-mail sales@arcadiapublishing.com
For customer service and orders:
Toll-Free 1-888-313-2665

Visit us on the Internet at www.arcadiapublishing.com

*To Elizabeth "Lizzy" Evans Harris, Anne Boula Bezdek,
Anna Bezdek Harris, and Dr. Judy Harris Helm.*

CONTENTS

ACKNOWLEDGMENTS

My family members were coal miners in southern Illinois from 1880 until the Great Depression in 1931. From 1911 to the present day, our family has lived in the village of Glen Carbon. Often, a village dependent on a single industry, such as coal mining, is abandoned after losing its livelihood. However, our village struggled and survived, which I attribute to the families who stayed and the leaders they chose to take care of the village.

Admiration for my dad, LeRoy J. Harris, and one amazing lady, Joan Foster, who initiated the saving of our village's history, really brought this book to print. Joan and her husband, Ronald J. Foster, mayor from 1979 to 2000, began saving history such as recordings, observations written by villagers, and donated artifacts. In 2001, Mayor Ben Maliszewski created the Glen Carbon Heritage Museum, where Joan and her group preserve the past. In addition, Joan was responsible for forming the Glen Carbon Historical Commission in 1988.

Saving history takes time. Ours began in the 1970s, when a room in the 1914 school building became a library with a display area for historical items. A new library was built in 1998, and the entire 1914 school became the Glen Carbon Heritage Museum. I would like to thank Jessica Mills and Samantha Doolin, coordinators of the museum, and the Glen Carbon Historical Commission for permitting me to explore their files and present their photographs.

My husband, Bob, is a patient man, and my grandson Eli Burns-Irvin is a whiz at photography. Photographs not otherwise credited are from the Glen Carbon Heritage Museum.

INTRODUCTION

In 1884, the village of Glen Carbon, Illinois, became a part of America's industrial revolution because of natural resources. The village is located among the eastern bluffs of the Mississippi River in the valleys of two forks of the moderately-flowing Judy Creek. Businessmen, looking for financial success, found the valley. The forested banks of Judy Creek proved to be a profitable place to open coal mines, as well as uncover clay for making good bricks. In addition, railroad builders liked the valley's gradually sloping surface.

Southwestern Illinois was already known as fertile farmland and was likened to the "Land of Goshen." The land surrounding Judy Creek supported large farms owned by the likes of Col. Samuel Judy, a Blackhawk War veteran and namesake of Judy Creek, and Nelson Montgomery, a Civil War veteran.

In the 1870s, the narrow-gauge Nickel Plate Railroad, hauling produce to St. Louis markets, discovered the gradual slope of the Judy Creek valley; soon, two more railroads followed. In the 1880s, a brickyard and three mines were built; the acrid smoke of burning coal, still remembered by old-timers today, lingered for 40 years. The population in 1900 when the mines were working was 1,200, but by the mid-1930s it had dropped to 300 when they closed for good. At that time, Mayor Frank Yanda Jr. had to turn off streetlights to save the village money.

In the early 1800s, a trail about two miles long led from the prairies south of Edwardsville to Samuel Judy's farm on Bluff Road. On the trail, in 1853, William Yanda built his blacksmith business. Yanda's location soon attracted other trades, such as a wheelwright, a watch repair shop, and a shoemaker. The incorporation of the village in 1892 surrounded these early businesses, and the trail became Main Street.

The slight downhill grade from the prairies to the American Bottom allowed freight trains and streamliners to build up earth-shaking vibrations as they traveled full-throttle toward St. Louis. I remember the shaking of the house every time one of the streamliners made the curve on the track a block away on the Illinois Central Railroad.

By the time I came along in 1940, my coalminer grandfather Roy Harris had been laid off, and my father, LeRoy Harris, was working at Hopcroft Electric out at Glen Crossing. The "boom town" image of the village had changed to a quiet Main Street with wooden buildings slowly being destroyed by age and uselessness. The village had an education district of its own: No. 83. High schoolers rode busses to Edwardsville District No. 7, but the younger children were fortunate enough to be educated by caring teachers right here in the place they lived. During these years, schools instilled hometown pride in children. Churches were active, and the villagers were often given a taste of togetherness by the celebrations of the holiday seasons with public singalongs and treats from the American Legion. Boy Scouts, 4-H clubs, the Kiwanis, and Teen Town entertained the young people. Over a span of 20-plus years the village remained somewhat isolated, but still close enough to larger towns for necessities.

In the 1930s, Mayor Yanda planned a water system, which was put in after his death. In the 1950s, land northwest of the village was bought up to build the Edwardsville branch of Southern

Illinois University. After losing its economic support in 1931, the village became a bedroom town for workers in the area.

When the 1960s brought the first subdivision to the village, the mayors and trustees had the foresight to create a comprehensive plan for the future growth of the village. Citizens held homecomings to fund parks, and historical photographs were rounded up along with stories from older citizens. The beautiful Ronald J. Foster Heritage Trail was built on the former Illinois Central Railroad right-of-way, the 1910 village hall was saved, and the 1914 school became a museum.

"Old Town" is now in the center of 77-plus high-quality subdivisions and commercial areas. The village has access to several state highways and an interstate. Old Town has two of its buildings designated as national historic sites, and Main Street has been preserved as a local historic district.

The mayor and trustees, with minimal commercial support but with a strong comprehensive plan, turned Glen Carbon into one of the "Best Places to Live" on CNNMoney's list of America's best small towns in 2009. The Glen Carbon Centennial Library was named the Bill & Melinda Gates Foundation's "Best Small Library in America" in 2010.

One

BEGINNINGS

Before the Village of Glen Carbon was incorporated in 1892, its location was already marked in history. In 1799, southwestern Illinois was called the "Land of Goshen" by Rev. David Bagley. The Land of Goshen included the Mississippi River floodplain "American Bottom," across from St. Louis, Missouri, settled by farmers who found the rich bottomlands profitable. Samuel Judy, a Blackhawk War veteran, moved from the settlement of New Design near Kaskaskia to the Land of Goshen and bought a farmstead from Ephraim Conners. In 1803, he built a large two-story brick home along Judy Creek, a substantial creek exiting the bluffs into the American Bottom.

In 1853, Austrian blacksmith William Yanda immigrated to the St. Louis area and settled in the Judy Creek valley. He built a log home for his family and opened a blacksmith shop on a two-mile trail that ran between Edwardsville and Samuel Judy's land on Bluff Road.

Railroads found the slope of the Judy Creek valley ideal for routing their tracks toward St. Louis. The first railroad was the Nickel Plate, built around 1874. It was joined by the Clover Leaf Railroad in about 1883. By this time, the industrial revolution had begun in the United States. Shale clay to produce building bricks was found buried beneath the bluffs along Judy Creek, and bituminous coal used to produce energy was found 90 feet below the surface.

In 1883, the St. Louis Press Brick Company built seven kilns to produce bricks. A few years later, in 1889, William E. Guy, president of the Madison Coal Company, opened three coal mines and bought property in the valley. Guy platted the valley with streets and rows of single-family and two-family saltbox-type houses. Businesses soon followed to accommodate the additional coal mine workers.

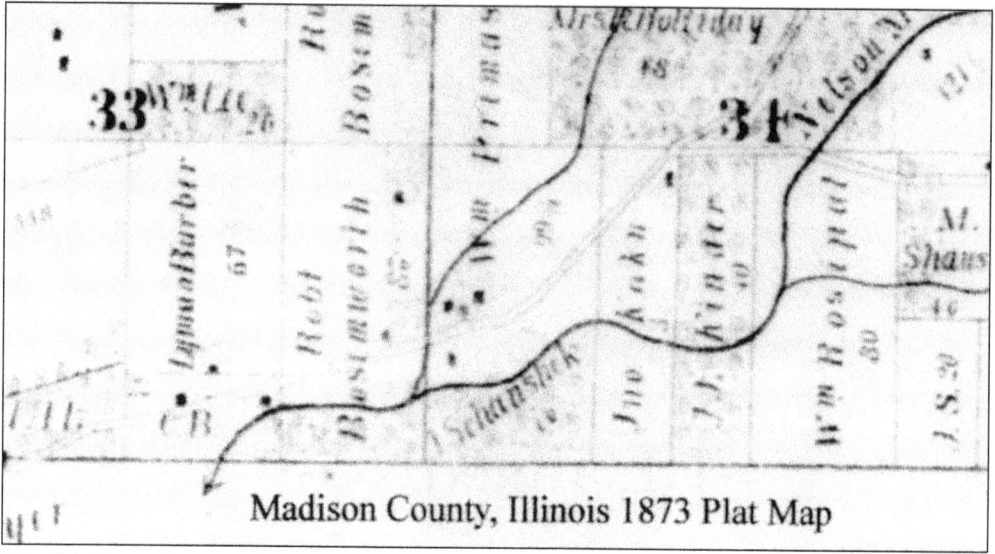

Madison County, Illinois 1873 Plat Map

This Madison County plat map from 1873 shows the location of William Yanda's blacksmith shop as two small squares at center. The small symbol between the squares is a crossed hammer and tongs, indicating a blacksmith. The dark line is the course of Judy Creek. Faded double lines indicate the future Main Street.

This is a tintype of William Yanda's blacksmith shop on the trail in 1885. The newer addition on the front of the original Yanda home was a saloon. The log home on the right no longer exists. The Yanda family, with 11 children, is listed on the 1870 US Census under the name "Yander."

The Yanda log cabin, built in 1853, is 32 feet long by 18 feet wide and divided into two rooms. The cabin, a local landmark, has been preserved by the village. Events honoring pioneer life are held there, such as when the Yanda family was honored by the National Society of the Colonial Dames of the 18th century.

THANK YOU

BOB WILLIAMS AND VOLUNTEERS

FOR RESTORING

THE YANDA LOG CABIN.

1989-1992

Bob Williams restored the log cabin from 1989 to 1992, along with volunteers Joyce Williams, LeRoy Harris, Mike Palmer, Bob Jones, Ed Masterson, Pete Perry, Blandford Smith, Stan Stimac, Ken Trebing, John Trebing, Jim Grover, Lonnie Cook, Herman Barker, Chris Burns, Jim Burns, L. DeConcini, Joan Foster, Ron Foster, Joe Glockner, Joe Griffin, Ann Harris, Buddy Harris, George Harris, Robert Harris, Dynel Harville, Steve Henson, Caine Kelso, Jessie Lyle, Susie Makler, Bill Newman, Marilyn Sulc, Dennis Williams, Mike Williams, Don Williams, and R. Williams Jr. Additional support was provided by the Bechtal Corporation, Kiwanis Club, Jaycees, Old Towne Tavern, First Baptist Church, and Glen Gardeners.

The 1992 village centennial quilt is being sewn by volunteers in the restored Yanda log cabin. From left to right are Laurabelle Harris Huser, Joyce Harris Williams, Ovella Wein, Erwin Wein, and Anna Bezdek Harris. The center motif is the village's logo.

Pictured is the east room of the restored Yanda log cabin. Bricks from the St. Louis Press Brick Company have been embedded among the limestone rocks of the fireplace.

Village historian LeRoy Harris is pictured at the remains of the foundation of the tower house in the 1980s. To the left is the Nickel Plate Railroad. Behind him on the right is the Illinois Central Railroad right-of-way. The Clover Leaf Railroad is out of frame to the left.

The interurban electric streetcar tracks cross the Illinois Central (IC) Railroad at Glen Carbon Crossing. Streetcars ran through Glen Carbon Crossing and on to Litchfield for coalminers working in local towns. In 1933, it was replaced with Illinois Route 159. Today, the Ronald J. Foster Heritage Trail runs through a tunnel under the highway.

The 1906 railroad tower house was manned 24 hours a day to receive telegraph messages. The operator made sure the directional switches on the tracks were pointed in the right direction to avoid wrecks.

Pictured here is a 1920s Nickel Plate train wreck at the tower house. The front of the engine is on the right, and the remains of the tower are in the center. No one was injured. The wreck was caused by too much speed on the downgrade from Edwardsville.

The Nickel Plate Railroad's steam engine No. 730 pulled coal and passenger cars. Later, diesel engines replaced steam engines. This photograph was taken at the South Main Street crossing in the village.

Sitting on a railroad work car are Henry Liebig (left) and Louis Krumick at Peter's Station siding in front of a work shed. In the background is a grain elevator with parapets around the top; the offices are in the buildings to the right. A cornfield is also visible at right. This impressive-looking elevator was preserved until 2019, when it was dismantled. The building of the elevator was noted in a 1920 issue of *Co-operative Manager and Farmer* magazine: "The Progressive Grain Company of this place and Peters will build a new elevator and expect to have this plant ready to handle the 1920 wheat crop."

The 1906 IC railroad depot was at the south end of Collinsville Street. The track was originally named the St. Louis & Eastern Railroad before being sold to the IC. The house on the hill behind the depot belonged to Madison Coal Company mine manager Mr. Daezner.

The 1890 Clover Leaf Railroad depot was on the west side of the village between the Clover Leaf and Nickel Plate tracks. The Mine No. 1 building and coal cars can be seen in the background. The original track was narrow gauge, hauling produce from local farms, and was changed to standard gauge in 1885 when it began hauling bricks from the brickyard.

The IC's steam engine No. 480 is pictured in 1903. The locomotive was used only around Mine No. 2 to haul cars filled with coal to be weighed at the Madison Coal Company headquarters. The old engine was a workhorse, shuffling empty and full cars on the tracks around the mine.

This display of railroad memorabilia at the Glen Carbon Heritage Museum includes the photograph of the Clover Leaf depot seen on the previous page and a railroad crossing warning sign with blinking red lights. (Photograph by Eli Burns-Irvin.)

The *Edwardsville Intelligencer* newspaper reported in 1893, "The main track was competed late Tuesday evening, after which the workmen, 130 in number, went to Marine's Turner Hall and were treated to an elegant supper by President W.E. Guy. After supper, a procession was led by Mr. Guy and L. Kolb, our faithful worker, to whom most of the success is due. The Marine band, about 100 citizens and the laborers, with burning torches marched to the first train that ever crossed Marine's grand prairie, and after three cheers the train left for Glen Carbon." Rights-of-way of two railroads became part of the Madison County Transit (MCT) network of bike and hiking trails: the Nickel Plate in the west valley of Judy Creek, and the IC in the south valley.

Five-inch-square decorative brick was made by the St. Louis Press Brick Company of Glen Carbon. This type of brick was used in decorative work, usually on the front of buildings. Bricks made by the company include plain narrow patio, white fire, toplined paving, and plain common. (Both photographs by Eli Burns-Irvin.)

Seen here is a 1909 Sanborn fire insurance map of the Glen Carbon St. Louis Press Brick Company. Shale clay clumps were brought to the central part of the brickyard, where they were crushed and screened for impurities. The clay was pressed into various brick molds, then taken from the molds and stacked with space left around each brick to air dry in "Brick Dry Ho," as shown on the map. When ready, the bricks were taken to one of the 12 kilns. The bricks were again stacked with space surrounding them. Each kiln was connected to an underground tunnel and to a fire pit. The fire was made with wood or coal. The large chimneys would provide a draft for heat to circulate in the kilns and bake the air-dried clay bricks to rock hardness. This map was drawn before the brickyard suffered a large fire in 1906, which destroyed the buildings; the brickyard was not rebuilt. Remnants of tunnels were found underground when the brickyard was dismantled. The bricks in the tunnels were burned several shades of red, orange, and yellow because of the extreme heat (1,500 degrees and more) passing through them. The IC Railroad sidings are now part of the MCT trail. Mine No. 2 was a quarter mile south of here along the tracks. Broken bricks can still be seen in Judy Creek where the MCT trail crosses it.

Shale clay is being removed from a bluff in 1883 by a clamshell excavator. It is retrieving columnar shale clay, visible directly below the digger at center. The clay traveled via narrow-gauge railroad to the brickyard processing plant, a quarter of a mile northeast of the "pit." Historically, clay for building brick houses was dug from creek banks. Shale clay is best for bricks; the consistency of the clay before firing is like the clay used to make pots and vases. The bricks that were used to build early houses were made on the site of the construction. A fire pit was dug, with a long tunnel to provide draft.

Brickyard workers stand in front of one of 12 kilns rebuilt in 1895 after a fire. The *St. Louis Post-Dispatch* reported on April 15, 1895, "The St. Louis Pressed Brick Company suffered a loss of $200,000 by the destruction of the works at Glen Carbon, Ill." The men are removing bricks from the kiln and putting them on a conveyor belt to be moved to a loading dock. Bricks were used for paving, lining steel-making furnaces, creating decorative facades for buildings, and laying sidewalks. The process of making a brick was about 10 days from digging the clay to completion.

Pictured is a brickyard worker's union ribbon for the International Brick, Tile & Terra Cotta Workers Alliance, Local No. 9. This side is black, and the reverse is red. The black side was to be worn for funerals, and the red side for meetings. The *Edwardsville Intelligencer* reported on October 22, 1895, "The workmen in the yards of the St. Louis Press Brick Co, of Glen Carbon, have struck. . . . The trouble originated Friday when two men, members of the Brick Workers Union, were discharged. The local No. 9 Union asked and were told that they were dismissed because of lack of work. The members of the No. 9 left their work and went home. . . . A number of men from St. Louis arrived at Glen Carbon yesterday morning intending to go to work. They were seen by the members of Union No. 9 who explained the conditions and persuaded them to return to St. Louis. . . . The Press Brick Works are owned by the Niedringhauses. . . . As high as two to three hundred men were employed at one time. Last spring the plant was destroyed by fire. Since it has been rebuilt about 75 men have been employed." The brickyard workers went back to work, and the brickyard hired more workers, as can be seen in ads in the *St. Louis Globe-Democrat* on September 11, 1904, seeking 25 laborers and "two shooters to shoot clay."

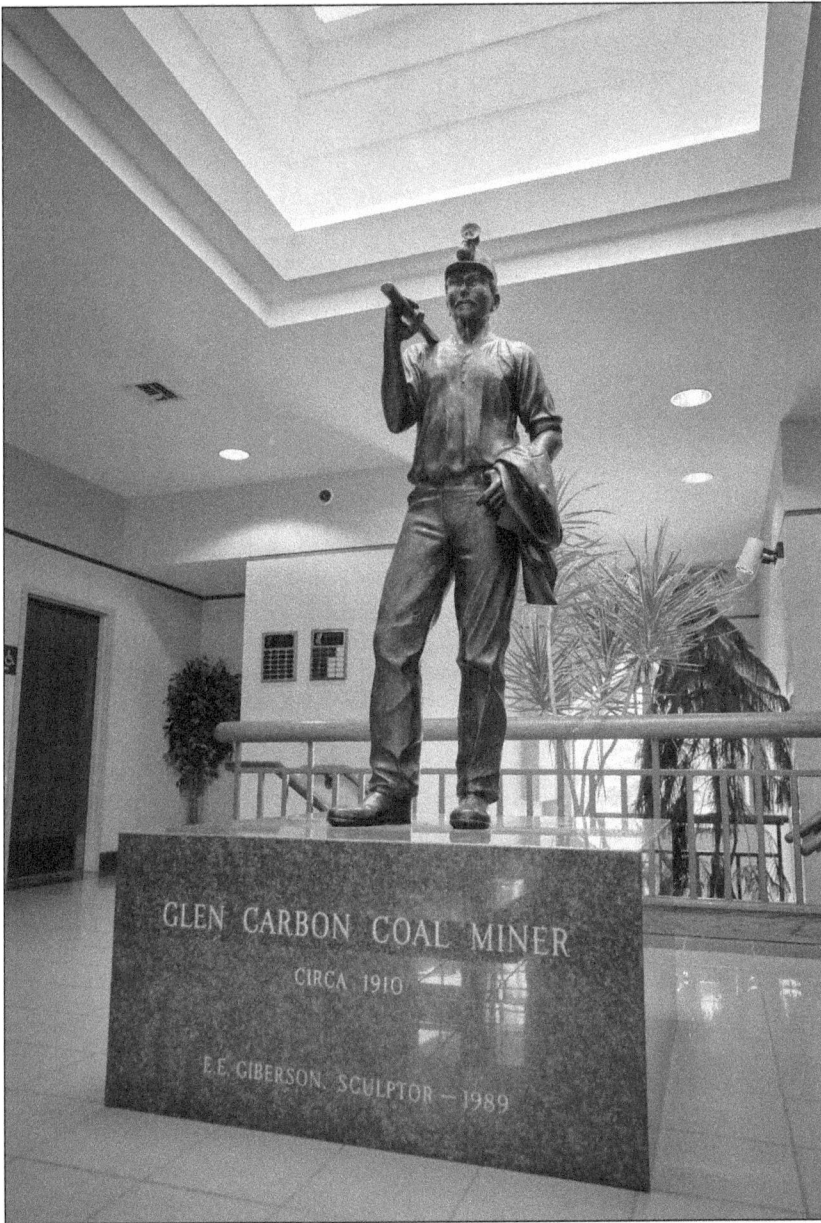

This bronze sculpture by E.E. Giberson depicts a coal miner around 1910. It was commissioned in 1989 by the Village of Glen Carbon to honor the heritage of the village founding. Mine No. 1 operated from 1890 to 1897, Mine No. 2 from 1891 to 1931, and Mine No. 4 from 1898 to 1914. The devotion of the mayors and boards of trustees and support by the citizens from the time the mine closed is responsible for the village of today. When the mines closed, coal miners could live free in their houses, and in 1936, buy them. The old town portion born during the heyday of the coal mines is surrounded by 77 subdivisions added and regulated by the village. They are all attractive and proud additions to the village. The village fathers have provided water and sewer, safety, and recreation for the people. There are 13 miles of bike trails, four public parks, and pocket parks maintained by the village, making it a great place to raise a family. (Photograph by Eli Burns-Irvin.)

Coal miners are seen in Mine No. 2 in the 1920s when the production of coal was greatest. Riding an electric car powered by batteries are, from left to right, Ed Smith, Garbalde Raffaelle, and Louis Trebing. Coal mining ceased in Old Town in 1931 but continued sporadically until 1950 along Bluff Road (Illinois Route 157).

This photograph of Mine No. 2 shows boilers and smokestacks in the background; the building contains a blacksmith shop, a machine shop, and showers for workers. A tipple is in the center with large wheels for elevators to bring coal up and take workers down into the mine. Stacks of wooden props for the mine tunnels are on the left. On the right are loading shuttles for loading coal onto IC Railroad cars.

Mine No. 4 was northeast of Mine No. 2, about one mile along the IC Railroad. In the background are the interurban streetcar tracks (Illinois Route 159). Mine Nos. 2 and 4 met underground. This image shows an elevated loader carrying coal to be emptied into IC Railroad cars.

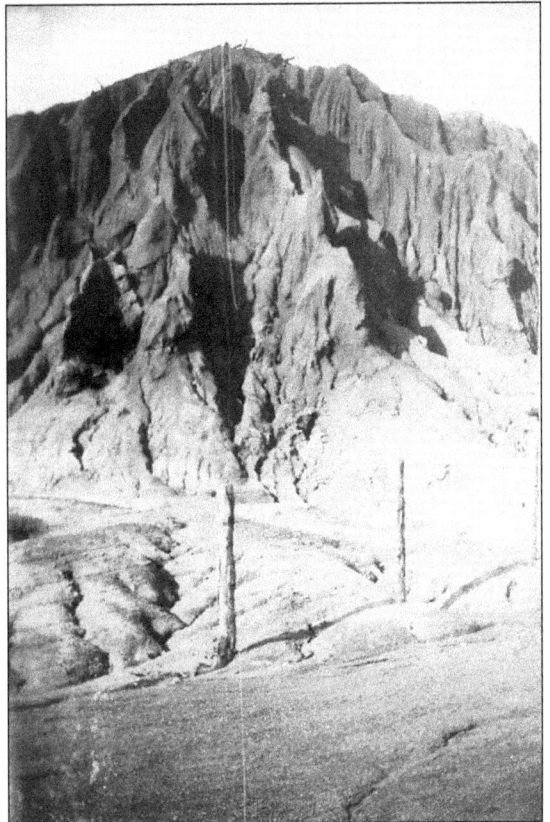

Remnants of coal "fines," pieces of coal not large enough to sell, accumulated into a slack pile about 50 feet high east of Madison Avenue. This 1926 photograph was taken before the pile was dismantled and used for fuel at schools and hospitals during a 1950s coal strike. Sulfur smoke vented from the lower layers and colored the soil orange. There are no remnants of the pile today.

Pictured here is a coal miner's heavy cloth working hat with a carbide lamp attached to the front. The coal mines were dark, but some weak light may have come from lamps hung on support logs or from strings of dim electric lights in a line down a coal tunnel. However, the miners in the small rooms off the main tunnel had no light. The first personal lights used by coal miners were candles, followed by small coffee pot–shaped metal containers with oil-soaked rags in the chamber and a wick sticking out the spout. Later, carbide lights were powered by dripping water onto pieces of calcium carbide in the bottom chamber of the lamps. When the marble-sized pieces of carbide combine with water, a gas is emitted that burns with a bright white light. The brightness of the flame could be controlled by a valve.

Seen here is the surface area of Madison Coal Corporation Mine No. 2 in 1907, with workers, visitors, and a mule. Mules were used below ground to haul coal cars. The mine shaft is on the right and was dug 90 feet deep into the Herrin vein of Pennsylvanian Period coal deposits, which are 300 million years old. The coal is bituminous, or soft coal, and is found in deposits 10 to 477 inches thick. (The mined seam averaged 5.5 feet thick.) Coal miners from all over the world came to the village to work. Slavs from Austria, Russians, Italians, Germans, and Americans from other parts of the country worked in the mines. Approximately 6,000 men worked in the Glen Carbon mines from 1895 until 1931. Most were single, but others raised their families in the village. Their descendants live here today.

The Illinois mine rescue car is pictured parked at the Madison Coal Corporation Mine No. 2. The car was deployed to mine disasters and was present at first-aid competitions. Each mine had a mine rescue operation team. The Mine No. 2 team took first place in 1930 in both state and international competitions. The teams consisted of volunteer coal miners. A group of Glen Carbon spectators stands in front of the safety car.

This is a photograph of typical coal mining tools used by miners. The pick and shovel are common, and the large drill makes the holes in the wall of coal to be filled with dynamite, which, when detonated, breaks the coal into chunks that can be loaded onto cars. The Glen Carbon Heritage Museum has more information on the use of these tools. (Photograph by Eli Burns-Irvin.)

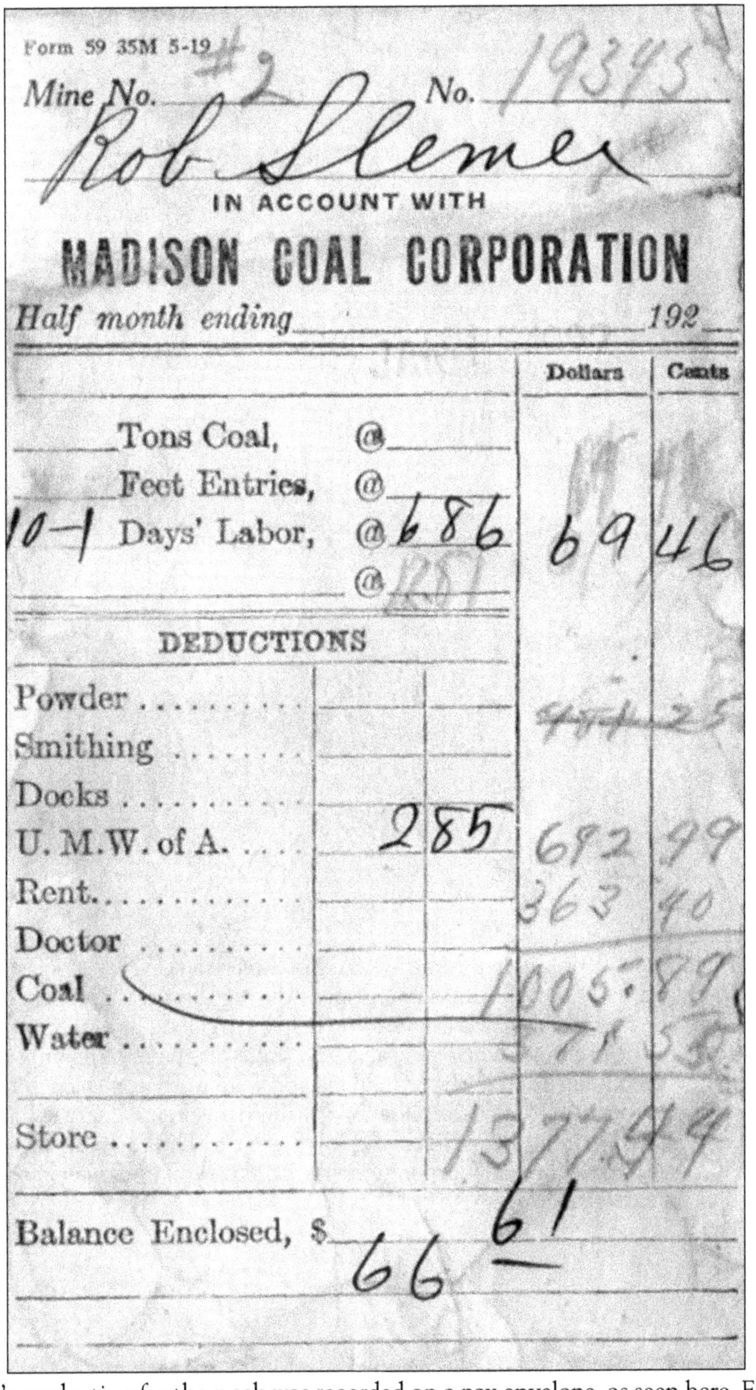

Form 59 35M 5-19

Mine No. #2 No. 19345

Rob Slemer

IN ACCOUNT WITH

MADISON COAL CORPORATION

Half month ending_____192___

		Dollars	Cents
____Tons Coal, @____			
____Feet Entries, @____			
10-1 Days' Labor, @ 686	69	46	
@			
DEDUCTIONS			
Powder			
Smithing			
Docks			
U. M. W. of A.	285	682	99
Rent.............		363	40
Doctor			
Coal		1005	89
Water		71	58
Store		1377	44
Balance Enclosed, $ 66	66	61	

Each miner's production for the week was recorded on a pay envelope, as seen here. Expenses for food, clothing, and fuel were subtracted from the wages. Payday kept the village running. Coal miners worked hard, and some felt they deserved to spend part of their wages on drinking whether they had a family or not. As a result, a few coal miner families had to suffer. Work was sporadic; the mines would stop working if there were no cars to fill or the lift was broke, and the workers would stop work in sympathy when a neighboring mine was on strike.

31

No. 686, the local union of the United Mine Workers of America (UMWA), organized on May 13, 1894. It interfaced with workers and management during disputes, kept wages even, and collected 25¢ dues at every meeting. Miners needing help buying food or with prolonged illness could always come to the union for help. They also held funds for the retirement of coal miners. The striped ribbons seen here are red, white, and blue and were worn at meetings; the back was black, to be worn at funerals. No. 686 got along with the Madison Coal Corporation and did not experience any hostility from the president A.J. Mooreshead. The company owned 12 mines in 1931 when it closed. Madison Coal Corporation was well known for its safety programs, even being awarded for its safety measures.

Two

INCORPORATION

The *Edwardsville Intelligencer* reported on June 8, 1892, that the election to organize the village of Glen Carbon took place the day before at the two-story brick school building. William Bosomworth, Jas. H. Lister, and George H. Bonsack acted as judges, and George C. Little and Joseph Maisch were clerks. Of 88 votes cast, 75 were for and 9 were against, with 4 not counting. "The returns were made known to Judge Wm. H. Krome this morning and were canvassed with the assistance of Justices E.W. Mudge and John Hobson, and the result found as above stated, whereupon said territory was declared to be duly incorporated, to be known henceforth as the Village of Glen Carbon. An election has been ordered to be held Friday, July 1st, for the purpose of electing a president and six trustees and a village clerk." Lister, given the duty of naming the village, suggested Glen Carbon, meaning "valley of coal." The village stretched along Main Street from Troy Wagon Road to just beyond the Clover Leaf railroad crossing on the west. The board appointed a treasurer, Irwin E. Little; superintendent of streets, J.B. Fallcetti; and a police magistrate, O.D. Oberlin. The board of trustees and mayor were to be elected by public vote each year. The police magistrate served for four years. Mayors Ben Weiler (1931–1933) and Frank Yanda Jr. (1933–1939) were serving when the mine shut down. Mayor Yanda at one time reported that there were "not enough funds to keep the streetlights on." Water procurement addressed in Yanda's term was put in by the Works Progress Administration in the 1940s. Later, mayors and trustees approved a sewer system and a comprehensive plan addressing planning and zoning. William Kleffmann, a citizen volunteer, wrote grants for parks and bike paths. Village citizens donated memorabilia and recorded events to preserve the history of the village. The village is a prime place to live, with its parks, hiking and biking trails, and police department and fire district. The population grew from 1,200 in 1900 to 13,000 in 2000.

Glen Carbon's first mayor is depicted here. As reported in the *Edwardsville Intelligencer*, "George Bonsack, the first president of the village, will be 26 years old October 7th next. He was born in St. Louis . . . then left for the west, where he worked with railroad and construction companies for about five years. He has travelled. . . . And is a young man of much practical knowledge and experience. He came to Glen Carbon from Black Hills, South Dakota. . . . His election was an eminently fine one and augers well for the thriving manufacturing village." (Courtesy of ancestry.com.)

Seen here are the homes of coal miners on Summit Avenue before 1910. Most families were Italian, thus its name, "Little Italy."

This is an 1895 view of the village from the west. Main Street is on the left, and Sunset Street is the long center street.

Seen here is a view of South Main Street in the 1910s. On the left is Chid Henry's Saloon and Primas Bakery, now the Glen Carbon Centennial Library. Four of the original six saltbox houses remain today.

This photograph of the intersection of Main and Collinsville Streets in 1910 shows the mercantile store, Rasplica residence, the Odd Fellows Hall and post office, DeConcini's Tavern, and Lawson's Restaurant. Schroeder's meat market is in the background on the right.

This Fairbanks scale was installed on May 16, 1899, in front of the Primas Bakery. In July 1899, a total of 915 loads were weighed, and $91.50 in fees were collected; the village received $45.75 of the fees. Here, Jean Neutzling (right) and two other women are leaning on the scale.

Three

POLICE, FIRE, SCHOOLS, AND HEALTH

The village grew, adding 77 subdivisions. The police force increased in 2020 to 45 personnel. In 1893, the first jail and fire department building were erected on the north side of Main Street, on the slope behind the American Legion. The small buildings are marked on a 1909 Sanborn map.

The first official fire department was organized in 1901. Charles Henry, Jim Stehman, Joseph M. Smith, H.L. Groeteka, and fire chief Frank Yanda were elected. In 1901, a man-powered cart with hose and buckets was housed in the wooden building on Main Street. In 1910, they were moved into the village hall with hand-drawn equipment. In the 1920s, the fire department bought a Ford Model T fire truck; it served until 1941. The fire department became a fire district in 1955, which is separate from the village. It was formed with a $40,000 bond issue for station No. 1 with two fire engines. Today, the fire department has two stations, EMT service, and specialized trucks.

A senior citizen center is located behind the village hall on North Main Street. There are several programs that bring relief to people looking for rides to appointments, help with taxes, and food services. A senior citizens' group made up of community members meets at the center.

Citizens serve on committees that keep watch over the operations of the village. Today, water, sewer, parks, and historical departments as well as several community advisory boards for citizen input and guidance are part of the government. Water was brought to the village in the 1940s, and sewers came in the 1970s. The grass is cut, flowers are planted, and parks are all taken care of by the village. Preservation efforts have resulted in the formation of the historical commission, caretakers of the heritage museum and the renovated Yanda Log Cabin, staffed by the village.

Two properties have been recognized as national historic sites. The Old Village Hall and the 1914 school are anchors of Old Town, along with the unique small homes and saltbox structures.

This is a portrait of a distinguished-looking Louis Weiler in 1899 when he was elected police chief. He was also hired to light the oil lamps along Main Street. Chief Weiler collected many fines of $3 for disorderly conduct in the local bars. Fines were collected for drunkenness, disturbance of the peace, and a few cases involving women who argued over their back fences, which ended in the "act of soiling the fresh laundered clothes hanging on the line by wiping dirty hands on such clothes." Later, as cars and trucks came into use, fines were assessed for speeding down Main Street. The badge proudly worn by Weiler is on display at the museum.

In 1910, the Oswald brothers of Alhambra, Illinois, built the Glen Carbon Village Hall at the corner of Summit Avenue and School Street, with a fire bell tower on the roof. Firefighting equipment was kept on the first floor. The upper floor was used for board meetings and village business. The basement was used as a jail for the police. The 1910 village hall is now a national historic site. In 2018, the historical commission nominated the building, and Will Shashek led the restoration. Volunteer William Kleffman found a replacement bell that rings every hour during daylight. (Photograph by Eli Burns-Irvin.)

The police department moved to its own state-of-the-art complex behind the village hall in 2004.

A child stands in the driveway next to the original fire department and wooden jail. Formed in 1901, the fire department used the building with open doors to house its equipment until the construction of the 1910 village hall. The driveway is located where today's American Legion building sits.

This is the original motorcycle ridden by Officer Jones. It was the first of several in the department. In addition, there are two four-legged canine officers on the force. The motorcycle is on display at the Glen Carbon Heritage Museum.

The 1991 police department stands in front of Glen Carbon Village Hall. The new police headquarters included a community room. Currently, 40 personnel are aided by two canine officers and are involved in public services for children and needy citizens.

A firefighter's helmet and coat are on display at the Glen Carbon Heritage Museum. Property taxes of residents in the Glen Carbon District fund the fire department, which is made up of paid personnel and trained volunteers, who can be called at a moment's notice. The present fire district has two stations manned by 36 members including four paramedics and four EMTs. The department holds open houses and gives tours to schoolchildren throughout the year. (Photograph by Eli Burns-Irvin.)

On January 18, 1898, ordinance No. 60 was passed establishing a fire department in the village. W.A. Daech was appointed chief engineer, and Jas H. Lister was named assistant chief engineer of Glen Carbon Chemical Fire Company No 1. The 1912 volunteer firefighters pictured here are, from left to right (first row) Frank Yanda and Ned Stenham; (second row) Rudy Primas, William Wieduwilt, and Frank Ricker. The men standing in the third row are unidentified except for J.B. Jones, ? Miller, Jules Schiller, and William Heck, in unknown order. An expense for $447 was listed at a subsequent board meeting for a half payment to Western Fire Engine Supply for a "Chem Engine and Handcart with 600 feet of hose."

Fire department volunteers stand in front of the 1910 village hall; from left to right are Aurie Primas, Bill Henry, Ray DeConcini Sr., Don Schiller, John Wendzenski, Jack Koch, John Allaria, Lorraine DeConcini, Walter Wydra, Joash Critchley, John Schiller, Lester Hardy, Ben Neutzling, and Al Ricker. The Glen Carbon Fire Department went from being the village's responsibility to a taxing district in 1955. Prior to the fire district being formed, the fire department was made up of devoted volunteers, with expenses paid by the village. The men not only helped fight fires, but also took care of other emergencies.

The 1910 Glen Carbon Village Hall is a national historic site. The white flag seen here features the logo of the village honoring its coal-mining history. The lower level of the hall is presently used by the Metroeast Model Railroad Club, which built a detailed diorama of the village and its railroads. (Photograph by Eli Burns-Irvin.)

The firemen seen here are Jack Cook (left) and William Heck at the entrance to the 1910 village hall, where the firefighting equipment was kept. In 1910, the village fire department purchased its fire truck, chemicals, and hoses. The two tanks held foam for spraying onto flames. The hoses in the center and the buckets stacked on the sides of the carts were used for water. Today, the equipment looks primitive and not very effective. But the men who manned the water hoses and carried the buckets risked their lives, just like the firefighters of today.

In the late 1890s, the state office of education assigned District No. 83 to the village grade school and Smola one-room school. District 83 schools educated 500 children from 11 foreign countries as well as the United States. The children's ethnicity was approximately 37 percent American, 17 percent German, 17 percent Slavic, 16 percent English, and 10 percent Italians in 1900. Originally, the main school complex in the village included a single-room school; a two-story, two-room brick school built in 1890; and a third wooden building with four rooms and two stories built in 1893. The one remaining brick building constructed in 1914 served through the 1950s. Glen Carbon schools consolidated with Edwardsville District No. 7. No longer needed as a school, the 1914 building was purchased for $1 and used as the village hall, with offices, police department, and a small library and museum. When the present village hall was built, the 1914 structure became the Glen Carbon Heritage Museum. (Photograph by Eli Burns-Irvin.)

During its centennial year in 2014, the brick school was listed in the National Register of Historic Places. (Photograph by Eli Burns-Irvin.)

Seen here is the village school complex on School Street, on a large square lot donated by the Madison Coal Company. The small white building was the first, then the 1891 brick building and the 1893 impressive white clapboard, two-story, four-room building followed. Madison Street intersects with Sunset Street at the back of the property.

Built in 1909 on land donated by Zephanian Montgomery, the Acme School was east of Glen Crossing on Troy Road. A second room was added in 1919. The school closed in the 1950s when Edwardsville District No. 7 was organized. The class of 1919 is pictured here.

The 1913 Smola School was located at Peter's Station. Early settlers Samuel Judy and William Whiteside had established schools in this vicinity. The brick building sits near Norma's Produce on Illinois Route 157 at West Main Street. This image is from a 2017 *Edwardsville Intelligencer* article. (Courtesy of Paige Maag and the Glen Carbon Historical Commission.)

The 1918 Glen Carbon class is pictured in front of the 1914 brick school building. From left to right are (first row) Elmer Kleine, Raymond Wieduwilt, John Anderson, Frank Pelligrini, Carl Groeteka, Henry Schneider, Albert Raffaelle, and Leo McCollum; (second row) Freida Rukadot, Anna Bertoldie, Anna Foucek, two unidentified, Coila Beckman, Lydia Miller, and Esther Tessler; (third row) Mary Sasek, Grace Pizzini, Anna Roskie, Frieda Schroeder, Agnes Smola, Isabelle Fisher, Rose Pizzini, Leona Krumeich, and teacher Lillian Eads; (fourth row) Ben Williams, Ben Neutzling, Joseph Unger, John Peradotti, Tom Nekola, John Ferris, Clyce Shashek, and Wilson McManicule.

A parade celebrated the final day of school in 1912. The drum corps led, followed by the school principal wearing a crown, with children behind him. Each class made a banner carried by a randomly picked student, who took their job seriously. The parade ended at Henry's Park on Main Street, where each student received a ticket for ice cream and soda. The upper grades distributed the treats, which was also an honor.

In 1939, a committee raised funds for a bus to transport village students to Edwardsville High School. From left to right are Bill Rasplica, Lizzy Harris, Herminia Shashek, Mary Hardy, Myrtle Titter, and Mayor Frank Yanda. Bus drivers included William Rasplica, LeRoy Harris, a Miss Schroeder, Jim Going, and Mamie Wieduwilt. Joe Cunningham, a volunteer, is quoted as saying "anything from a nickel up will be acceptable" to raise the $1,200 needed.

This photograph was taken in 1926 in Boulder, Colorado. That summer, these Glen Carbon schoolteachers drove to Boulder for classes and brought so many clothes that they barely had room to pack shoes, according to Helen Kenner. From left to right are Jennie Rafaelle, Kenner, Mamie Casna, and Jennie Miller. The teachers left an impact on their students, including sisters Marguerite and Irma Henry. Kenner said fathers told their daughters, "boys or books," so they chose books, and their students were rewarded. They also chose Eastern University, not necessarily for quality education, but because they could ride the Nickel Plate Railroad for $8 per round trip. The high level of education taught in the village has produced men and women proudly serving as educators, scientists, political leaders, artists, and others. In 1990, Dr. Nick Holonyak Jr. received national honors for his work with semiconductors. He praised the education he received when he attended the village school.

The 1953–1954 fifth-grade class was taught in the 1895 two-story wooden school building, with Bethel Silva as the teacher. This was the last year for classes in the old school, as the building was torn down the next year. Only the 1914 brick building remains as the Glen Carbon Heritage Museum.

Bethel Sliva's 1954–1955 fifth-grade class is seen in the new elementary school. On the right from front to back are Mary Jo Henry, Mike O'Hara, Judy Harris, and two unidentified. In the first row with the sign on her desk is Pat Poneta, and left of her in the black dress is Mary Jane Weckman.

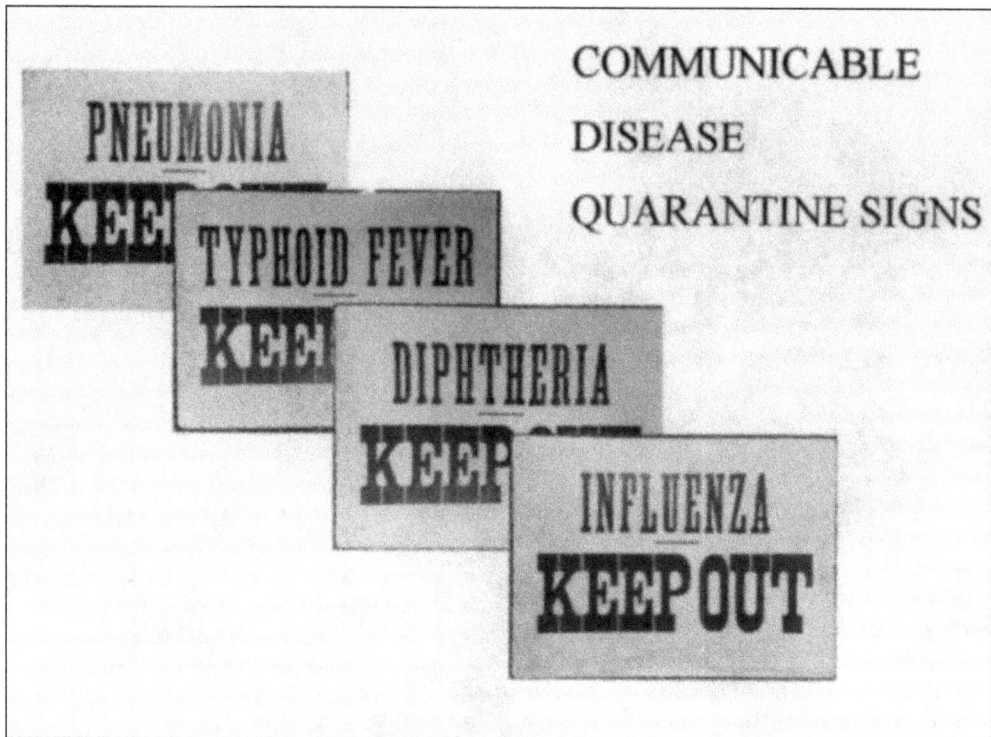

Warning signs were put up when communicable diseases were found in the village in 1915. Strangers were not allowed to enter. The villagers' health was cared for by Drs. Oliver, Kirschner, and W.E. Range during the prosperous years of 1890–1931. After the Depression, out-of-town doctors would come to Glen Carbon to care for elderly patients and to work with local midwives to deliver babies at home.

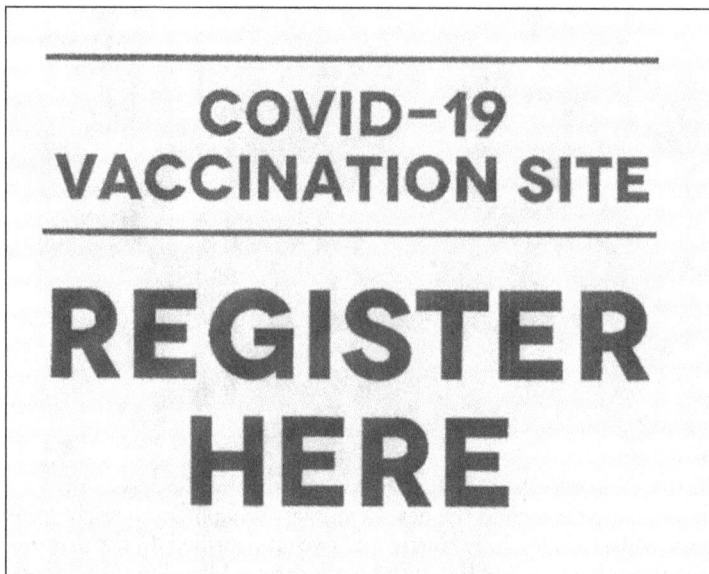

The 2020 COVID-19 outbreak in the United States caused most citizens to quarantine for a year. The CDC implemented guidelines for the public to follow to stop the spread of the disease. Wearing face masks was mandatory, restaurants closed, and social gatherings were limited to a few people. At least 500,000 Americans died before a vaccine was available.

Four

OLD TOWN BUSINESSES

The brickyard and coal mines in 1883 and 1889 brought businesses to the area along Main Street from Glen Crossing Road to the Judy Creek bridge on the west side of Old Town. At Main Street and Glen Crossing Road, the Primas family is preserving Primas' Saloon and Aurie's Primas Garage. Remnants of Dom Pizzini's Western Brewery Depot, built in 1904, and his house remain on the west side. At the curve of Main Street is the renovated blacksmith's residence, the 1853 Yanda's log cabin. Across from the cabin, Old Towne Tavern (built in 1895) and two 1885 saltbox houses remain. Today, Jamie Wilkinson has built the new brick Wooden Nickel Bar and Grill where Allaria's Store and Christ Schroeder Bros. Meat Market were located. Today, across Main Street, Groteka's 1922 brick building contains Karma on Main and Shear Grace Hair Salon. On the same side of Main Street are lots that contained H. Lister/Weiduwilt and Sam Berger's store. The Lister/Weiduwilt wooden building burned in 1919, and Birger's Leader brick store (built in 1893) survived until 1950. Today, next to Wieduwilts and Birgers, is an original saltbox residence. Following that is a surviving 1890s wooden building with a sidewalk overhang used historically as a doctor's office, Lawson Restaurant, Midway Cafe, and a snow cone shop. Today, the building is preserved by the Henry family. A 1922 brick house and store built by the Tessler family survives today. American Legion Post 435 now occupies the space of the 1903 Knights of Pythias Castle Hall. The Rasplica residence (built in 1903) is being preserved by the family. Today, Miner Park is entered where the company store Dooner's Mercantile (built in 1890) stood. The village gazebo and 2002 centennial library are located where the 1890s Primas Bakery stood. It was also used as the village post office until the 1960s. The library sits where Chid Henry's Saloon and Imaginary Theatre was located. The 1976 covered bridge honors Glenda Kovarik, a longtime city clerk. Along the south side of Main Street are the original 1892 saltbox and family houses. Next to Judy Creek was Schneiders Drayage and stables.

Honored by *CNNMoney* in 2009 as one of the best small towns in America, the article stated, "Glen Carbon's name reflects its mining heritage. This town half an hour from St. Louis has abundant vegetation and a soothing view of the Mississippi River basin." Old Town stretches for four blocks along Main Street. It is home to a mixture of businesses and residences today, as it was 123 years ago. (Photograph by Eli Burns-Irvin.)

Pictured here is the middle part of Main Street today; on the left is the Old Towne Tavern, still in business, and on the right is the sign for the Yanda log cabin, home to the pioneer blacksmith who first settled on Main Street when it was a trail in 1853. (Photograph by Eli Burns-Irvin,)

56

This view looks down Main Street, 30 feet in elevation higher than the lower section. On the left behind the trees are residences including some new houses and an old saltbox two-story house. The right side shows the remains of Dom Pizzini's Western Brewery Depot and his saloon with a porch; both are now residences. (Photograph by Eli Burns-Irvin.)

The Wooden Nickel Pub and Grill and other smaller businesses on Main and School Streets are located where the 1890s Allaria's Store once stood. It is part of the preservation of Old Town; note the style of the brick building. Up School Street is the 1910 Glen Carbon Village Hall, which is listed in the National Register of Historic Places. (Photograph by Eli Burns-Irvin.)

This saltbox residence at mid–Main Street, erected in the 1890s, is alongside Lawson's building, which was used as a doctor's office, a restaurant in the 1930s, and lately, as a snow-cone business. It is being preserved by the Henry family. (Photograph by Eli Burns-Irvin.)

An event is being held at the Primas/Bluff Saloon, built around 1891 on Main Street at Troy Road. A buggy at far left is being pulled by a long-horned steer. A buggy pulled by a horse is followed by a wagon with windows on the side (possibly a funeral wagon). The property is being preserved by the Primas family. The Sedlacek and Stehman Soda Factory building on the right no longer exists.

58

Primas Garage, built in 1927, is next to Primas' Bluff Saloon. Aurie Primas was running the garage when this photograph was taken. This building is also being preserved.

The Western Brewery Depot, built in 1904, was run by Dom Pizzini, shown delivering barrels of beer to the many taverns on Main Street. Pizzini is on the wagon, leaning against the beer barrels. The building's first floor survived and is now a residence.

These bottles are from the Sedlacek and Stehman Soda Factory. Built in 1908, it was also known as the Glen Carbon Bottling Works. The factory was next to Primas' Saloon on Glen Crossing Road. (Photograph by Eli Burns-Irvin.)

This is a photograph of Christian Schroeder's meat market in 1891 on Main Street. Schroeder wears a white apron. Conditions in the village were described as "raw"; Mrs. George Schneider, whose husband in 1892 ran a stable and hauling business next to the creek on Main Street, said it felt like she had moved to an uncivilized place when she moved to the village, as reported by her daughter Lucy in an interview at age 97.

Inside Christian Schroeder's meat market in 1900, hams and sausages are on the counter in front of, from left to right, Christian Schroeder, Anton Schroeder, Johnny Evanko, John Wesley Seaton, William Kirchoff, and John Sido. Christian's brother Anton became a partner in 1896 and they changed the name to Schroeder Brothers.

Two young ladies stand in front of the Odd Fellows Hall on Main Street at Collinsville Street. The space was used by William Rasplica as a general store, and it was the village post office in the early 1900s.

Charley Wieduwilt's barbershop was in William Wieduwilt's Palace Saloon building in 1910. Charley Weiduwilt (left) and Bill Daniels are the barbers; the customers are unidentified. Regular customers had their own shaving mugs, seen on the wall.

The first Odd Fellows Hall (built in 1890) was across from Primas' Bluff Saloon. Winter's Hall, on the top floor, was used for the first village board meetings, and the bottom floor was the cooperative store known as Singletary's.

62

Patrons are pictured at William Wieduwilt's Palace Saloon in 1899. Wieduwilt is at center behind the bar, his daughter Mamie is behind the bar at right, and his son Charley stands at the bar in front of his sister. Mamie Wieduwilt is fondly remembered in Glen Carbon. After her father died, she ran a restaurant and ice-cream shop in the Yanda building. She lived in a house her father built on Main Street that still stands as a residence today next to the Wooden Nickel. At the house, she took care of her elderly mother, raised a son, and made a living hauling coal and other things in an old pickup truck. She took care of the old white Methodist church for years. She was respected and admired as she made her own way in the village.

Pictured are patrons of James Lister's Saloon in 1896. The village was home to numerous saloons. Coalminers were hard workers; they did not get paid much money, but what they did earn seemed to be spent at saloons on the way home from work, as can be seen by some of the men's clothes. The man in the vest leaning on the bar at right is William Wieduwilt, who bought the saloon and building from Lister. The man at center appears to be holding a chicken.

Old Towne Tavern, presently a business on Main Street across from the Yanda log cabin, operated as a tavern since the early 1900s. It was built by Frank Yanda Sr. in the 1890s. The patrons in this photograph were probably coalminers after a day of work. Things did not always go well in the early governing of the village; when the village was incorporated in 1892, it collected a "dram shop" license fee of $500 per year or $250 for six months from saloon owners. All seemed to go well except for Frank Yanda Sr.'s saloon; the village had to use legal action to collect his license fee, according to 1892 village board minutes. The village received funding from county and state taxes and collected its own tax of $1 per dog. One hundred dogs were tagged per year from 1893 to 1918.

Pictured here is Vincent Allaria's delivery truck for his grocery business on Main Street. Allaria is at far right in the hat; his son Tony, who worked at the store, is behind the wheel of the truck; and his son John is standing on the fender and spare wheel. The truck is parked in front of their house at Glen Crossing in 1920s. Vincent originally followed his father Dominic and became a coal miner for a while. His father was a superintendent at Mine No. 2 in 1919. Vincent opened his grocery store on Main at School Street in 1920. The Allaria family's story is like many in the village: Dominic moved his family to the village when he took the coalminer job. His son Vincent followed him in the mines, and the family lived in Glen Carbon through the Depression.

In this image is the interior of Allaria's grocery store on Main Street; Vincent Allaria is standing at center, and his son Tony is behind the register. The woman is unidentified. There were several small grocery stores in the village; however, they carried everything from potatoes to sewing material. They had merchandise in cases, on the floor in barrels, and hanging from the ceiling. Allaria's store, like Schroeder's larger meat market down the street, allowed coalminers' families to run up bills to pay later, even during the Depression. Note the very large cash register with the fancy sides and back; these were common in early stores.

Three young women sit on a hitching post on the side of Gus Pizzini's Saloon on Main Street in the 1920s sporting fox-fur wraps.

William DeConcini is behind his bar in a two-story wooden building on Main Street in 1903. Located next to Castle Hall, it burned in 1919. The DeConcini family stayed in the village. After the fire destroyed the business, DeConcini did not rebuild the structure. The lot stood vacant and is now used by AT&T. After the mines closed, businesses closed, leaving empty buildings on Main Street. Only the undertaker was left, and he worked out of the miners' co-op store, which shut down. Small stores could not stay open; however, most of the taverns did not close. On Main Street, east of School Street, a bowling alley was located in a building right on the street; it closed, but the house in back remains today. The Steibert Restaurant operated in one of the houses; it also closed, but the house stayed. The house next to Old Towne Tavern is believed to be a log cabin; it was the home of Mayor Frank Yanda Jr. when he served the village.

The DeConcini family is pictured here in the early 1900s. From left to right are William Jr., Raymond, Joseph, Albert, and mother Teresa. Raymond served as the leader of Local 474 for 60 years before retiring in 1982.

Seen here is a pyramid-roofed miner's house, typical of the single-family homes built for the coal miners to rent. This residence is on Sunset Avenue. (Photograph by Eli Burns-Irvin.)

Pictured here are patrons at Frank Premor's saloon on Main Street. From left to right are (first row) Al Spoeneman, Fred Weiler, "Captain" Richards, Eli Lever, and Riley Strong; (second row) Frank Premor, Jim Bradley, and Ed Valine. There was a party going on, as they are all dressed in their best clothes. These men were not shop owners; they worked in the coal mines.

This is a view of the side of the Primas Bakery building on the northwest corner of Main and Collinsville Streets. It was one of the first businesses built in the village about 1893. Bakery goods were brought from Edwardsville in the beginning. Ovens were in the back of the building.

This capital stock certificate for one share of the Glen Carbon Co-operative Society belonged to Leo J. Wydra. Each share was worth $10; this one was sold on August 10, 1925, and was signed by William Henshaw, secretary, and Joash Critchley, president. Shareholders were allowed to shop at the co-op store in the village.

Seen here are members of the village Unemployed Council at a soup cookout on August 31, 1931. The members are, from left to right, (first row) Lizzy Harris, Charlie Klein, and Purse DuVal; (second row) unidentified and Mealie Smith; (third row) a Mrs. Critchly, Delta Snow, and Joe Cunningham; (fourth row) Minnie Barney, Mamie Wieduwilt, and Ann Evans.

This was one of the original 1890 buildings on Main Street; today, the library is on this site. To the right is the Primas Bakery, and on the left are apartments. Children sit on top of a scale for weighing wagonloads of goods. Each time the scale was used, the village got a portion of the charges.

In this 1914 image, Lucy Schneider is doing what she wanted to do all her young life: work in the Primas Bakery across Main Street from her father's drayage company. She married an older man, and they did not have any children. When interviewed at the age of 97, Lucy told interviewers of her wish.

This image was captured during an 1890s celebration of the Czechoslovakian National Society at Myers Tavern and Dance Hall at Glen Carbon Crossing. Immigrants from Austria and Slavic countries were drawn to the Glen Crossing area, where many of them had relatives. Glen Crossing was annexed in 1917. To the left (or front) of the building were the tracks of the interurban electric streetcar system that ran through Illinois towns, starting at East St. Louis and running through Collinsville, Maryville, Glen Carbon, Edwardsville, and Litchfield. The streetcar service stopped when the Depression hit. The tracks were removed, and Illinois Route 159 was built in its place. In the foreground where the young man is standing is the Glen Crossing ball yard, now a funeral home, and Meyers Hall is now a dentist's office.

Ray Kubicek is in front of Meyers Hall at Glen Crossing in the 1940s. The car is a 1930s model with front-opening "suicide" doors.

A man is pictured delivering flour and other necessities to houses on Sunset Street in 1895. The four-wheel light "buckboard" wagon had a driver's seat on springs attached to the bed of the wagon.

This image was captured inside Chid Henry's Main Street Saloon; on the right is owner Chid Henry. Joe "Vino" Caviglia, at left, was a coal miner, born in 1888 in Coal City, Illinois. His father died and his mother moved to Glen Carbon and married coal miner Joseph Zadra. She died giving birth to their first child. Joe was 14 in the 1900 Census. He did not get along with his stepfather, so he left Glen Carbon and returned in 1906 as a transfer coalminer from Belleville. Caviglia became a favorite among the young ladies in town and can be seen in photographs at several social outings. He served for three years as a village trustee, and was a regular on the Maroons baseball team in Glen Carbon. During a Glen Carbon mine shutdown, he moved on to Sesser, Illinois, as a coal miner and baseball player. He married and raised a family, and his granddaughter Allison Caviglia Barash currently lives in Pittsburgh, Pennsylvania.

Four young men are enjoying their buckets of beer on the back porch of an unknown saloon in the village. From left to right are Jimmy Laulis, Rudy Schiber, Buck Hubbard, and Fritz Hersching. Laulis is holding the top section of a gramophone. These spring-operated musical recording players were quite popular.

The Wayside Inn building is pictured including the 1895 Steis Addition on West Main Street. The "sports" on the porch were patrons of the saloon.

Five

PEOPLE, MUSIC, AND BASEBALL

Homecomings with fireworks and, lately, Glen Fests are part of today's village gatherings, held on Main Street and in Miner Park. The Yanda log cabin and the heritage museum hold smaller public gatherings. Organizations of village citizens and some church groups work to keep the village active and attractive. The churches have not changed and are very active, holding services on Sundays along with weddings, funerals, and Bible schools during the summer. The leisure time in the past was spent with music, dances, and baseball. Today, one can add hiking and biking to the list. Weddings are as important as ever and are usually between village residents, as in the past. Some of the earlier weddings between local young people include LeRoy Harris and Anna Bezdek, Ray Kubicek and Katie Schiller, William Rasplica and Isabelle Weiler, Sylvia Williams and Arnold Trebing, Joan Treat and Ronald J. Foster, Bunny Douglas and Lillian Nicolussi, Laurabelle Harris and Fred Huser, and Peter Perry and Blanche Sisk. Couples were often neighbors who met at the old Coal Park on Austin Avenue or at ballgames, but more likely, they met at a local dance. The music in the village ranged from German bands, jazz bands, and Czech bands. Dances were held at Meyer Hall at Glen Crossing, Imaginary Theatre, St. Cecilia's Hall, or on "one of the best floors to dance on," according to an old-timer, the second floors of buildings on Main Street, especially the one used by the Coal Miners Union. Village churches have worked out a schedule for public suppers: Catholics put on chicken dinners, Episcopalians have pasta dinners, the Methodists have soup and bread nights, and of course, there is the fish fry at the American Legion every Friday. Today's gathering places in Old Town include Old Towne Tavern, Taco Tuesdays at the Wooden Nickel, Weeping Willow lunches, and food and drink at the Cabin. The commercial area surrounding Old Town has a variety of cuisines available.

This image was captured during a village homecoming in Chid Henry's Park in the 1950s, with the Imaginary Theatre in the background. The hall had been a silent movie theater and dance hall. Most importantly, this is where the grade school picnics at the end of the year were held. Good food and games of chance were the highlights for the adults.

Homecomings raised money for local groups and were enjoyed by the whole family and looked forward to each year. The area around Imaginary Theatre is home to the library now. The village opened public parks, starting with Citizen's Park, the coal mining–era ball park. Main Street was even closed off for homecomings and Glen Fests every year.

Teen Town met in the 1914 public school, and this dance was held in the Imaginary Theatre. The group spent time cleaning it up for the dances. Kneeling in the striped shirt is Joan Trebing Calahan. Emma Dawson is one of the scrubbers, and standing second from left in the white dress and directing the work is Carol Munzert.

Teen Town was active during the 1950s and 1960s. The village's young people were not able to participate in many of the events at the Edwardsville Senior High School because of a lack of transportation. Churches had youth activities. The Catholic Youth Organization and the Methodist Youth Organization were two of the most active groups. The Kiwanis Youth Committee sponsored trips to events and swimming pools in the summer.

Four young boys graduating from eighth grade are pictured at a school picnic in 1914. A band member is in the second row, directing them. Every year, the school classes would march from the grade school to Henry's Park on Main Street and be treated to soda and ice cream.

4-H Club members are ready for an outing in 1949. From left to right are (first row) Charlotte Stoces, Loretta Klibeck, and Joyce Harris; (second row) Marilyn Belythe and Janet Ranek; (third row) Carol Rasplica, Velda Mae Primas, Phyllis Helfer, Pat Henry, and Teresa Raffaelle. The 4-H Clubs and adult women's home extension groups were branches of the University of Illinois Home Services in Edwardsville. Besides sewing lessons and food preparation demonstrations, village clubs explored local historical sites such as Cahokia Mounds in Collinsville and Fort de Chartres in Prairie de Rocher, Illinois. The best projects were taken to the state fair in Springfield.

United Mine Workers of America No. 686 gathers at Madison Coal Mine No. 2 in 1917 to sell war bonds. Mine officials and politicians gave speeches and met their quota. During 1917 and 1918, patriotic groups pushed to pay off the World War I debt. The union was a strong organization that worked well with the Glen Carbon Coal Corporation. It held regular meetings, collected dues, and paid its retirees. More than once, it helped women who came to them for money to feed their children.

In the 1950s, American Legion Auxiliary No. 435 served the Hod Carriers Union Chicken Dinner. Pictured are, from left to right, (first row) Mary Perry Thomas, Edna Miller, Mildred Mayer, Alice Henshaw, Florence Ingels, Norma Well, Isabelle Ricker, Emma Gibson, Mary Weiler, and Irma Weidzinsky; (second row), Lil Weiler, Ann Plessa Enos, Sally Cunningham Weiler, Dorothy Miller Wydra, Tessie DeConcini McGill, Mamie Wieduwilt, Loretta Leach Dawson, and Barbara Wieduwilt. Village women worked at dress factories in Collinsville, as maids in Edwardsville, and in area factories. The coal company sold the company houses to their workers for $50 a room. New families moved into the vacant houses and took root in the village; many of the families living in Old Town today came after the Depression. Mayors and trustees took care of the town and made it a good place to live. The economy boomed after the 1950s, surrounding Old Town with shopping centers and subdivisions.

Pictured are members of the Kiwanis Club of Glen Carbon in 1953. From left to right are (first row) Clarence Bohm, Ralph Well, Roy Green, Harold Smithson, and Nick Hamilos; (second row) Elroy Well, Edward Schroeder, Tom Shashek, Ray Winterburg, David Hammond, John Newman, Bill Newman, and Blandford Smith; (third row) Stan Stimac, William Rasplica, Mark Sedlacek, Robert Sedlacek, Garland Knight, Glen Seaton, and Larry Kacer. The Kiwanis, Knights of Columbus, Jaycees, American Legion, and other groups are the workforce behind volunteer projects for the village. Christmas singalongs, toy giveaways, Little League, and Boy Scouts were supported by groups like these. The launch of the Walmart shopping complex at Cottonwood was the first in the village. A few retail stores have opened in Old Town, and there is room for more. The village grows as annexations are added, making the village 10 square miles in size with a population of 13,000 and growing.

From left to right, Charles Burgdorf, Edgar Miller, and Pat O'Hare are pictured in 1922 on Main Street in front of William Yanda's soda parlor. Across the street are two saltbox houses. The 1910s and 1920s were years of regular work in the mines. Young people married, cars became a nuisance, and speeds had to be regulated as the village grew.

Sisters Mary Watson Kalal (left) and Katherine Watson Mateka are ready for a trip to St. Louis to the World's Fair in 1904. Young people took trips to the fair and beyond on one of the three railroads. The deports were busy with riders and gawkers, an old-timer said, and half of the fun was waiting to see who came to town and who was leaving.

In this 1910 photograph, Bill Bowen (left) and Archie Neutzling ride down "Church Hill," a favorite name for Sunset Street. Both were sons of coal miners and became miners themselves. Bowen lost a finger in 1930 due to an accident. Typical rental houses for coal miners are visible in the background.

Eddie Schmalbach (left) and Joe Vino are seen in the first row. They were 14 years old at the time, and listed in the 1900 Census as "at school." Behind them is Eddie's brother. All three became coal miners, traveling around the mines of Illinois and back to Glen Carbon.

The Arthur Neutzling seen here on a bicycle next to the family's Christmas tree in the early 1900s may be the same Archie Neutzling pictured on a bicycle on the previous page. The tree has lit candles burning on the branches; many a tree caught fire around this time. Other ornaments include cutouts of angels, dolls, and baskets, as well as glass balls.

This photograph was taken at a birthday party in the village, possibly around 1910. From left to right are (first row) Esther Tessler, unidentified, Al Raffaelle, Dorothy Collier, Lee Bradley, and Annie Piazzi; (second row) Grace Pizzini, Mabel Cross, birthday girl Bernice Bradley, Minnie Mae McCullum, Ione Valine, Bill Henshaw, Willis Schroeder, and unidentified; (third row) Arlene Dee, Irene Valine, Olinda Weiler, Elsie Bowen, Benny Williams, Henrietta Dee, and Grace Orr. Most were the children of businessmen in the village. Arlene Dee's daughter Henrietta had a small variety store at Main and Collinsville Streets that sold penny candy, material, and thread. She would let her customers "put back" an item and pay for it a little at a time. The store is now a vacant lot.

A highlight in 1912 was receiving an invitation to a party or dance organized by the society-driven ladies of the 1912 Club. They arranged fine dancing parties with orchestral music and the like; however, attendance was by invitation only. From left to right are (first row) Lucy Schneider Moore, Alice Henshaw Schriber, Sophia McLeod Lawson, Bertha Demmrich, unidentified, and Elizabeth Titter; (second row) Emma Schroeder Schon, Jennie Krotz Purtle, Bertha Whalen, and Julie Krotz Purtle. Emma was the daughter of Chris Schroeder, a storekeeper. The Krotz sisters' father had a large farm. Lucy got her dream job of working at the bakery; her father owned the Schneider Hauling Company and a stable on Main Street.

The wedding of Katie Schiller and Rudy Kubicek was held in 1912. The bride and groom are seated at left. Also seated is Florence Schiller. Standing are, from left to right, Minnie Kubicek, Joe Litner, Alvina Kubicek, Frank Kubicek, and Bert Evans.

These young people are playing "London Bridge" at Imaginary Theatre in 1910. From left to right are (first row) Gene Page, Jean Neutzling, Ora Primas, Joe Caveglia, Bertha Whalen, Blanche Miller, and Cy Henshaw; (second row) Chas Shashek and Tom Miller; (third row) unidentified, Florence Schiller, and Bert Evans. The stage curtain in the background features ads for local businesses.

The Glen Drum Corps is seen here in 1922. The members are, from left to right, (first row) Grace Pizzini and Pat Raffaelle (second row) Cecilia Beckman, Elizabeth Mayer, Blanche Sisk, Mamie Casna, and Frances Sisk; (third row) Victoria Subic, Elizabeth ?, unidentified, Jennie Raffaelle, Helen Kenner, Rachel Meyer, and Ella Critchley. Their coats were bright red, and their skirts were white; later, they also wore white straw hats. They formed the drum corps because so many of Glen Carbon's young men went to war. They told friends they could create music for parades and other events in place of a men's band. The group was well-known and was asked to play in parades in other towns. Several of the young women were teachers at the Glen Carbon School.

Members of Joseph Ladd and His Orchestra include, from left to right, Irv Dollinger, Jerry Stroud, Joseph Ladd, Art Dippold, and Udell Mason. Village children often slept on coats stacked in coat rooms on Saturday nights. Grandparents watched the children, while the dancers "cut a rug," including dancing with a broom. The author remembers her father grabbing a broom and starting to dance. He would approach a couple, tap the man's shoulder, and exchange his broom for the girl.

This image of the Old Five Keys band members includes, from left to right, (first row) Al Schleuter, saxophone; Joe Ranek, banjo; and Bob Kubicek, drums; (second row) Ray Kubicek, trumpet; and Ray Trebing, clarinet; (in the truck) Al Resbeck. Popular in the 1940s and 1950s, the Old Five Keys played outdoor events, including homecomings.

In the 1920s, a women's softball team played on the village baseball field. They are, from left to right, (first row) Gloria Svaldi Blakely, Jennie Svaldi Primas, Doris Koch, and Adele Wilkison Sliepen; (second row) Isabelle Weiler Rasplica, Helen Mateyka, Olive Svaldi Swanson, Helen Watsek, and Velma Primas Meoski.

The 1934 Glen Carbon School basketball team was made up of, from left to right, (first row) Jim Drew, Frank Poneta, Fritz Luksan, George Burian, Reese Evans, and Wilbur Dawson; (second row) Russ Treat, Al Ricker, Charles Barone, Joe Sladsky, Les Slemer, and coach Harold Helfer. Helfer, a coach and teacher, also served as mayor of the village. The Glen Carbon School District No. 83 had a hard time financially but was lucky to have dedicated teachers and board members. District No. 83 joined District No. 7 in 1955.

These 1910 Glen Carbon baseball team members are, from left to right, (first row) Elden Miller, right field; Joe "Vino" Caviglia, captain; Peter Weckman, catcher; and Ray Weiler, second base; (second row) Herman Hennings, pitcher; Alex Marshall, pitcher; Arch Evans, third base; Chas L. Henry, manager; John Shiller, left field; Ray Kubicek, center field; and William Liebde, first base. Some of the players wear Maroons uniforms (a Glen Carbon team), while the rest are wearing the uniforms of Central Brewery. Baseball was important in the village. These ballplayers were from different towns, and they learned their baseball skills as they traveled working in coal mines. Some stayed in the village, while others moved on to the next job.

This 1934 Glen Carbon team won the championship of the Southwest Illinois Intercity Baseball League. From left to right are (first row) Al "Lefty" Sedlacek, pitcher; Tony "Tonda" Unger, catcher; and James "Chick" ?, pitcher; (second row) William "Mop" Henry, outfield; William "Huck" Haywood, outfield; William "Hoot" Burgdorf, scorekeeper; Charles "Smitty" Schmit, infield; Frank "Hank" Unger, infield; and Lou "Stucco" Perry, infield; (third row) Ott "Fat" Pelligrini; Ray "Kubi" Kubicek, outfield; Charles "Motch" Biarkis, infield; Ed "Sticky" Meyer, manager; Charlie Wieduwilt, groundskeeper; and Hank Liebig, pitching coach. It seems all the ballplayers had nicknames; these are only a few on the list at the Glen Carbon Heritage Museum.

The champions of the Glen Carbon Kiwanis Little League are pictured here in 1969. From left to right are (first row) Terry Sedlacek, Tommy Sedlacek, Robert Pyles, Robert Ellington, and Lonny Dawson; (second row) Robert Kinamire, Steve Brockmeier, Dale Ethington, Jimmy Newman, and Larry Martin; (third row) Rusty Burian, Greg Smith, Hal Henson, and Don Perry; (fourth row) Blandford Smith (coach), George Burian (manager), and Joe "Pep" Sedlacek. Today, the Little League organization of Edwardsville and Glen Carbon is busy in the summer when several teams of different ages play. Glen Carbon had games at the old ballpark Miner Park, and newer diamonds at village hall on North Main Street. More ball fields are planned for other parks in Glen Carbon.

Six

THE VILLAGE

The faiths represented in the village in 1892 included Catholics, Methodists, and Episcopalians. Whether workers were from Europe or from North Carolina, they brought their faiths. Residents of today have added new faiths. Three cemeteries are associated with Old Town: City Cemetery (1901), Oaklawn (1850), and Buck Road (1867). They are joined by the 1800s Nix/Judy Pioneer Cemetery of pioneers from the Land of Goshen. Over 130 years, village citizens have served in two world wars and several other armed conflicts. Respect for their service is found at Honor Roll Park on Main Street in Old Town, just beyond the covered bridge.

The early village was built on clay bluffs denuded of trees. Houses were built on mud streets, and pollution from the mines stunted vegetation. Ninety years after the mines closed, remnants of the forests have returned, and the creeks have cleared. Parks in Old Town included a ball park and Miner Park, the result of a group of coalminers' children, including Charles "Chuck" Harris, LeRoy Harris, and Raymond Weiler going to the office of the Madison Coal Corporation on Collinsville Avenue in the 1920s and asking for a playground. It featured a gazebo, playground equipment, teeter-totters, a Maypole, and tennis courts. The park was dismantled in the 1930s. Today, Miner Park and Schon Park are the largest, with miles of bike and hiking trails throughout the village. The village had two men's baseball teams, Glen Carbon and Glen Crossing. Ball games were always played twice: once on the field and then in the local tavern. The village's 1895 ballpark became Citizens Park in 1999 and is today the entrance to Ronald J. Foster Heritage Trail. The village now has clean air and water. In the evenings, one may hear bats hitting balls or rhythmic tennis games. Walkers on the trails will see many birds and perhaps a deer.

A Methodist church was the first in the village, built in 1894 at 57 Sunset Avenue on a lot purchased from the Madison Coal Company. In 1983, the congregation was renamed New Bethel Methodist Church and moved to 131 North Main Street. The small white church on Sunset Avenue now serves the Shiloh Christian Church congregation. (Photograph by Eli Burns-Irvin.)

The New Bethel Methodist Church on North Main Street is named after the 1805 Bethel Meeting House marked with a monument at the entrance to the Lakewood subdivision. The same church has been active in the village since 1895 with youth groups and soup and bread dinners. On Tuesdays, the Quilters meet in the basement—their quilting skills are well known. (Photograph by Eli Burns-Irvin.)

The Episcopalians organized a congregation in 1905, and in 1912 built a church at 186 Summit Street. Coalminers from England formed St. Thomas Church in the village. The church is also built on Madison Coal Company land. St. Thomas's women hold a pasta supper every year and run a daycare for children. In the background is Main Street with an 1890s saltbox residence. (Photograph by Eli Burns-Irvin.)

The Edwardsville Church of the Nazarene built a new church at 400 North Main Street and named it Glenview Church of the Nazarene in 1978. The church holds an annual car show in its parking lot. (Photograph by Eli Burns-Irvin.)

St. Cecilia's Catholic Church in the village began with an Edwardsville St. Mary's Church priest holding Mass in the village school. In 1927, the St. Cecilia's parish formed and built a church with a bell tower and stained glass. Both were transferred to a new church in 1980 at 153 North Main Street. St. Cecilia's parishioners hold a yearly chicken dinner open to the public. The church is also a food bank. (Photograph by Eli Burns-Irvin.)

St. James Lutheran Church is on North Main Street across from the current village hall. The Glen Carbon church was established in 1982. Other churches once part of the village include the Assembly of God Church, which met in a small building on Main Street in the 1920s. The Baptists organized the First Baptist Church in the 1950s. (Photograph by Eli Burns-Irvin.)

The village has long honored those who served in wars. The Nix/Judy Pioneer Cemetery holds the graves of Revolutionary War veterans and the families of the farmers who settled in the Land of Goshen. The Glen Carbon Heritage Museum has lists of those buried in the cemeteries. The Nix/Judy Pioneer Cemetery is at the intersection of Illinois Route 157 and Interstate 270. (Photograph by Eli Burns-Irvin.)

The Nix/Judy Pioneer Cemetery overlooks the American Bottom from the west side of the bluffs west of the village. Some of those buried here include members of the Judy, Nix, Biggs, and Peters families. (Photograph by Eli Burns-Irvin.)

The Buck Road Cemetery, established in 1867, is on Illinois Route 162 directly south of the village. It is officially located in Maryville, Illinois. (Photograph by Eli Burns-Irvin.)

Oaklawn Cemetery, established in 1850 at Glen Crossing, was once known as the Barnsback Burial Grounds. Farming families east of the village are buried there, as are coal miners from the Glen Crossing area. (Photograph by Eli Burns-Irvin.)

The City Cemetery was established in 1901 on land purchased by the village board. It is in Old Town at the west end of Guy Street, overlooking the Judy Creek Valley and Main Street. The UMWA Union No. 686 purchased a row of grave plots for coal miners. (Photograph by Eli Burns-Irvin.)

This is a view of the eastern portion of the City Cemetery, an active cemetery maintained by the village. (Photograph by Eli Burns-Irvin.)

In 1922, a World War I doughboy memorial, currently located in the Glen Carbon City Cemetery, was erected to commemorate two local World War I soldiers killed in France: Harry G. Seaton (1895–1919) and Emil Trentaz (1889–1919). Funds for the monument, $1,045.86, were raised from a carnival, a dance, and donations. (Photograph by Eli Burns-Irvin.)

These young women, identified only as (from left to right) Rine, Tay, and Clara, donned uniforms in jest after their men had returned from World War I. Locals supported the war effort by buying war bonds and volunteering. The Red Cross organized groups of women at Glen Carbon Crossing and in Old Town to help make bandages and assemble other supplies for the troops.

During World War II, in 1942, Joan Foster (left) and Thelma Thomas do their duty by participating in a Junk Rally. A government document at the time read, "Don't let brave men die because we faltered at home. . . . Junk helps make guns, tanks, and ships for our fighting men." People were encouraged to collect and donate anything made of metal or rubber, including flat irons, rakes, bird cages, electric irons, stoves, light bulbs, bed rails, washing machines, farm machinery, lawn mowers, and even pianos.

A wood and brick memorial was designed by William Rasplica Jr. in 1944. The citizens of the village raised the money for the memorial, which contained 182 names of service personnel carved in wooden panels.

The original World War II memorial was updated to honor veterans of all wars and conflicts of the United States. In 2012, a committee created a beautiful park. The committee included Stacey Jose, chairman; Gary Hartzel, president; Ronnie Hicks, vice president; Joan Trebing Callahan, administrative assistant; and board members Dennis DeConcini, Kenny Hengehold, Steve Kaiser, Terry McKeon, Joe Maliszewski, Robert Olbrich, Michael Schonlau, Dave Noble, and Ralph Well. (Photograph by Eli Burns-Irvin.)

This image was captured during one of the annual marches honoring Memorial Day on Main Street in 2012, with members of the Glen Carbon Veterans of Foreign Wars 2222 and the American Legion Post 435, followed by the Boy Scouts of Troop 34.

The impressive full-service Glen Carbon Centennial Library, built to resemble coal mine architecture, is on Main Street next to the covered bridge. Beginning as a reading room in Cottonwood in 1975, the library moved to the village hall. In 2005, it became its own library district, and in 2009 was honored as the best small library in the United States. (Photograph by Eli Burns-Irvin.)

This is the village gazebo at the entrance to Miner Park in front of the Glen Carbon Centennial Library at the intersection of Main Street and Collinsville Avenue. Miner Park was the result of many homecomings sponsored by a citizens' group headed by trustee David Hammond. (Photograph by Eli Burns-Irvin.)

Miner Park is open every day from dawn to dusk. It has baseball diamonds, tennis courts with lights, a caboose commemorating the railroads, basketball courts, a dog park, and Judy Creek in the heart of Old Town. Bike riders often begin their rides from the park. Built with funds from a volunteer group, it has been part of the village since the 1970s. (Photograph by Eli Burns-Irvin.)

Judy Creek and Little League baseball fields are located in Miner Park. The trees in the background are on land that was once Mine No. 1. (Photograph by Eli Burns-Irvin.)

This caboose was moved into Miner Park in the 1970s. It is maintained by the Metroeast Model Railroad Club. A miniature model of the village and its railroads is set up on the first floor of the 1910 village hall. (Photograph by Eli Burns-Irvin.)

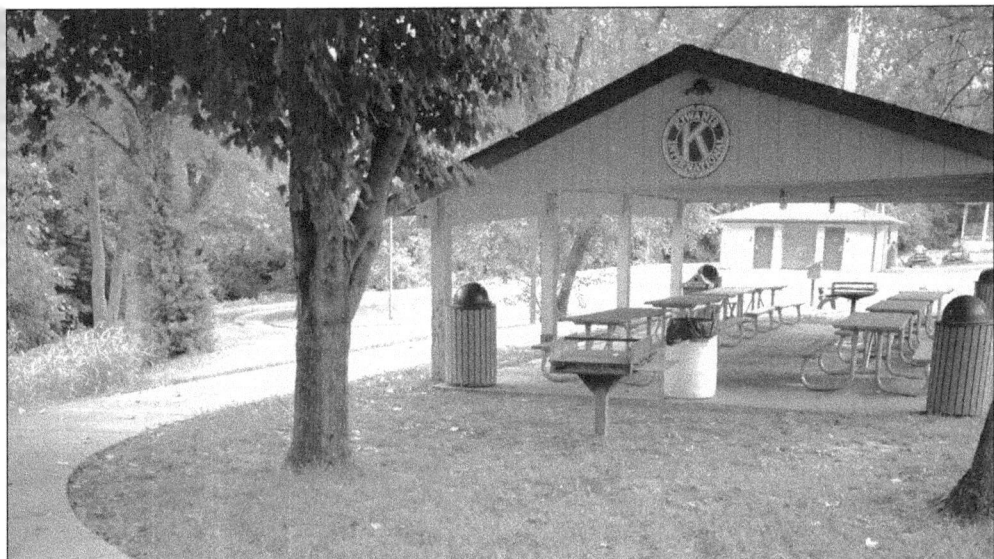

This picnic shelter in Miner Park was built by the Glen Carbon Kiwanis Club. The restroom building is in the background. There are shelters and picnic tables in Miner Park, Village Park, and Schon Park. (Photograph by Eli Burns-Irvin.)

Schon Park, across Main Street from the village hall, is still under development; baseball diamonds, tennis courts, and other facilities are planned. The parks in the village are the result of citizen generosity and the hard work of volunteers writing grants. (Photograph by Eli Burns-Irvin.)

The Schon Park walking path goes around the pond, on Main Street across from the current village hall. (Photograph by Eli Burns-Irvin.)

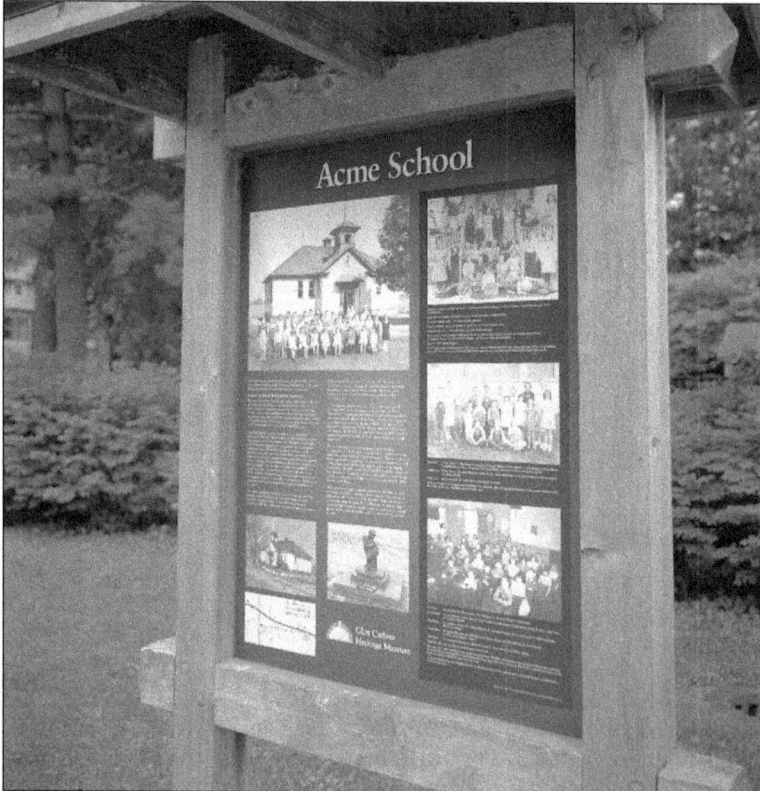

This is an information sign at the Acme School pocket park at Glen Crossing and Illinois Route 159. The Glen Carbon Historical Commission is responsible for the historical signs in Old Town. (Photograph by Eli Burns-Irvin.)

This Acme School pocket park statute honors the one-room schoolhouse in the Glen Crossing portion of Old Town and was dedicated by the Glen Carbon G.L.E.N. Committee of volunteers in 2012. (Photograph by Eli Burns-Irvin.)

This is a pocket park at the intersection of Main Street and Birger Avenue. The path leads to the Glen Carbon Elementary School on Birger Avenue in Old Town. The park is across Main Street from the Yanda log cabin. Several small resting places for hikers and bikers are present in the village. (Photograph by Eli Burns-Irvin.)

In 1991, the Ronald J. Foster Heritage Trail was created. The abandoned Illinois Central railroad was made into a historic trail by the addition of trail signs by Leroy Harris. The MCT Trail System took over maintenance of the trail in 2021 and honored the historical portion of the trails by having Carol Dappert and Joan Foster of the Glen Carbon Historic Preservation Commission suggest subjects for a new system of signs.

The 1976 commemorative covered bridge was built by volunteers. When Glenda Kovarik, a longtime village clerk, commented that the Main Street of Old Town deserved a covered bridge, she got her wish. It sits on Main Street at Meridian Road, adjacent to Honor Roll Park at the entrance to Fire Station No. 1. The first bridge was made of iron, and the second was made of concrete. The covered bridge was burned by a rambunctious motorcycle group as a prank a few months after it was completed, and volunteers rebuilt it. (Photograph by Eli Burns-Irvin.)

Seven

WHAT'S NEXT?

Of course, the wooden buildings of Old Town will not last forever. It would be nice, but alas, time will change the buildings; however, it will not erase the stories of how coal mines and a brickyard were responsible for creating a lasting testimony of immigration, economics, and the political mixture of the citizens. The citizens did not come from one place, one religious belief, one ethnic group, or economic situation—the Village of Glen Carbon began as a sum of all the above. There was no magic involved, just listening to one another's plans, working together toward goals, and the mindset of where they decided to live. The people would do their best to make it a good place for raising children, placing their heads at night, and the environment in which it all took place was worthy of keeping for future generations. Many residents of the village, in the comfort of their planned communities, do not know the village's history, so the Glen Carbon Historic Commission does its best to tell the story with exhibits in the Glen Carbon Heritage Museum and individual buildings that have been saved and turned into historical icons and museum exhibits. The mayor and trustees have followed up on the planning of new businesses and future subdivisions that will be assets to the village.

In 1989, the Yanda log cabin began a revival of preservation in the village. Volunteers led by Robert A. Williams, with the support of the mayor and trustees, began the project with enthusiasm. It put Old Town on the modern map. News about the restoration was big for the three years before the village's 1992 centennial. Today, the cabin staff provide education lessons for the Glen Carbon School across the street. It is a stop for bike riders and hikers as they ride and walk the trails through the village. With glass doors and lighting, it is possible to see the interior at any time. Pictures with Santa is a popular event, as is Cabin Day in the fall. (Photograph by Eli Burns-Irvin.)

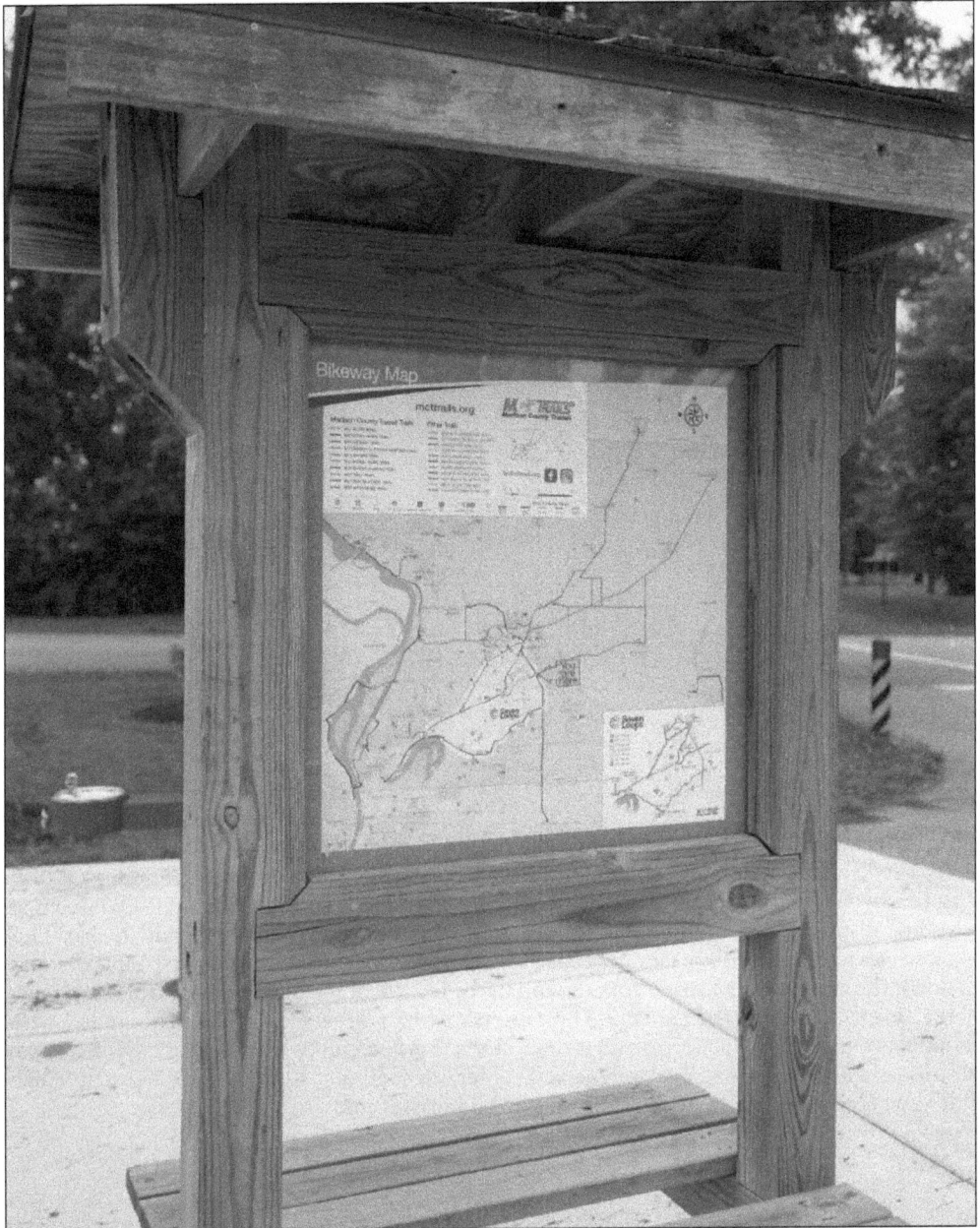

The village is the light-colored area in the middle of this map. The bike and hiking trail system began in Glen Carbon. Bill Kleffman, Charley Juneau, LeRoy Harris, and Mayor Ronald Foster began their project before the centennial. The IC Railroad right-of-way had been offered to the village as a conduit for water and sewers, but Kleffman brought the idea of "Rails to Trails" home with him after a trip to California. Harris, a native villager, saw it as an opportunity to tell the history of the village by erecting signs along the trail, and Juneau, an engineer, researched the trailbed. Mayor Foster, guided by Kleffman, applied for grants from the Illinois Department of Transportation for help with the funding. The Ronald J. Foster Heritage Trail became a part of a larger network when MCT began saving the network of rails through Madison County. (Photograph by Eli Burns-Irvin.)

This is a view of Main Street in the middle of Old Town today. Citizens have preserved the saltbox-style homes; four are seen along this stretch. The white fence encloses the preserved 1903 Rasplica two-story brick home. At this time, there is no national recognition for Old Town as a historic district. There are no railroads left, no coal mines open, nor a brickyard visible. This book strives to tell the village families that those places are not necessary for the people of today to honor the citizens of the past. Stories found in the records of the museum and exhibits of relics help residents remember their village. The east end of Main Street meets Illinois Route 159, with shopping centers and other stores and its own story; the west end of Main Street has a few small businesses with plans for a large commercial center across Illinois Route 157 to the west, which will also become its own story. (Photograph by Eli Burns-Irvin.)

William Guy platted two long streets along with Main Street running up the hill west to east. The second one, known as Sunset, runs from Judy Creek on the west to the No. 2 Coal Mine site to the east. On the left is the 1895 Methodist church, and along both sides of the street are many small four-room miners' houses. These homes today serve as starter family homes and homes for retirees, with some occupied for three generations of families that worked in the coal mines. There are several streets that run north to south off of Main Street. This is the intersection of Collinsville Avenue that leads to the south and the Madison Coal Company offices, still standing adjacent to the IC Railroad bike trail. Summit Avenue, at the top of the hill, has similar houses and the preserved 1910 Glen Carbon Village Hall. The south portion of Summit Avenue was known as "Little Italy." (Photograph by Eli Burns-Irvin.)

Anyone growing up in Glen Carbon either walked up a hill or down a hill, depending on where they were going. This is a section of School Street at the corner of Summit Avenue at the 1910 village hall. Main Street is at the bottom of the hill. One of the village's young entrepreneurs has invested in businesses along Main Street; this is a new brick and limestone building housing the Wooden Nickel Bar and Grill, along with a party room and a business office. Across from it on the north side of Main Street is a 1920 brick building with a dress shop and hair salon. At the east and west end of Main Street are small businesses; at the intersection with new Meridian Road and Glen Crossing Road is another of Jamie Wilkinson's buildings housing the Weeping Willow, a sandwich shop, and a new barbecue business. On the west end of Main Street is the library. Across the street are two mining houses that became a bike rental shop and a law firm. (Photograph by Eli Burns-Irvin.)

Located on the top of the bluffs, Wild Wood is one of the 77 subdivisions in the village. (Photograph by Eli Burns-Irvin.)

The Lakewood subdivision in Judy Creek Valley is home to the first Bethel church and cemetery, built in 1805. (Photograph by Eli Burns-Irvin.)

There are many hometown stories out there, and many longtime residents remember the acrid smoke of burning coal, walking to school uphill, and enjoying the log cabin. But in truth, Glen Carbon did not survive on its own—it had a lot of help from the elected officials who looked out for the water supply and sewers, volunteers who provided high school bus transportation, and those who continue to give their time to make it a wonderful year in Glen Carbon with Glen Fest, Cabin Day, Little League, and dancing schools. (Photograph by Eli Burns-Irvin.)

BIBLIOGRAPHY

"Best Places to Live: Money's List of America's Best Small Towns." money.cnn.com, 2009.

Clelland, David. *Historical Atlas of the River Bend Area, Illinois, 1819–1974*. Edwardsville, IL: Southern Illinois University, 1981.

Edwardsville Intelligencer, 1892–2021.

Engelke, Georgia McCormick. *The Great American Bottom*. St. Louis, MO: C. Sarne, 1983.

Foster, Joan, ed. *A History of Glen Carbon: Glen Carbon Illinois Centennial 1892–1992*. Glen Carbon, IL: Glen Carbon Centennial Committee, 1992.

History of Madison County, Illinois. Edwardsville, IL: W.R. Brink & Company, 1882.

Illinois State Geological Survey. isgs.illinois.edu.

Kipp, Louise. *History of Oaklawn Cemetery*. 1973.

Norton, William T., ed. *Centennial History of Madison County, Illinois and Its People: 1812 to 1912*. Evansville, IN: Unigraphic, 1970.

Sanborn fire insurance maps, 1902 and 1922.

St. Louis Post-Dispatch, 1890–1900.

United Mine Workers Union No. 686 minutes, 1894–1931.

Visit us at
arcadiapublishing.com